THE 60-DAY
CHALLENGE

ACHIEVING COMPLETE EMOTIONAL HEALING

(EXPANDED VERSION)

Drs. Dennis & Jennifer Clark

For video demonstrations and other teachings: www.forgive123.com

Visit our online school at http://training.teamembassy.com/

CONTENTS

WELCOME
to the
60-DAY CHALLENGE

Congratulations on your commitment to measurably improve the quality of your emotional and spiritual life. We don't want you to feel alone on this journey.

Those who respond to the Challenge are truly a special breed—hungry for more of God and willing to pay the price of Christian discipline. You are the very person that the Lord has been looking for. You, like Mary of Bethany, are choosing the better part that won't be taken away (see Luke 10:38-42).

I was the first one to embark on this quest with Dennis as my mentor and it was just the beginning of the most exciting and fulfilling time of my life. I can hardly even remember the pains and fears that were once my constant companions. The fruit of this extraordinary transformation has manifested in an absence of internal and external conflict and closer walk with God. I know that my testimony can become your story, too.

Pray along with the CD's and write in your journal immediately afterwards. Practice dropping down and forgive any offenses during the day. You may want to take Sundays off to reflect upon what you have recorded in your journal during the week and allow the Lord to touch your heart at your church. Be sure to keep a written record of all the Scriptures, words, and impressions that the Holy Spirit quickens. Enjoy the amazing quest that lies ahead!

Until I meet you in person,

Dr. Jennifer Clark

SECTION ONE

Spiritual How-To's

CHAPTER 1

SIMPLE PRAYER

The primary purpose of the *60-Day Challenge* is to help you draw closer to God. Dealing with troublesome emotions and thoughts is secondary, although very necessary for our emotional well-being. Therefore, we emphasize *daily* communion with the Lord in addition to *healing* prayer.

I (Dennis) was a young Catholic at the time I was saved. I knew little about prayer and how other people prayed but, when I closed my eyes in prayer, I *felt* the supernatural peace of God. Now, I had always been somewhat hyperactive, so peace of any kind was a new experience for me, much less the gift of supernatural peace Jesus gives to believers (see John 14:27).

Whenever something interrupted this peace (such as a negative emotion), I wanted to return as quickly as possible. I became acclimated to "touching" His peace and living in that atmosphere. Because peace is a gift given to believers by Jesus Himself, I understood that it was always available. All disruptions, therefore, were caused by me breaking my connection with Him. My times of prayer did not consist of talking to God. Instead, I enjoyed His presence—touching His divine nature. Later, I read many books on prayer, but by that time, I was so addicted to just being *with* the Lord that I only had one petition and that was for more of Him. As a matter of fact, I discovered that in seeking God Himself alone, He always gave me what I needed so I never needed to pray for "things." The Lord became my *"exceeding great reward"* (see Gen. 15:1).

My guiding scripture verse was Philippians 3:10 from the Amplified translation of the Bible, *"that I may know Him."* Years later I began to read Protestant books on prayer, and was confused because there was so much talking involved. Convinced that my first approach, simply to enjoy being with the Lord, was so much more satisfying, that settled the question for me.

Simple Prayer. Simple Prayer is prayer focused on adoring and glorifying God alone. It is based in the simplicity of a life-giving relationship with the

Lord. We spend time with Him and He imparts life to us. Paul admonishes us as believers to avoid being *"led astray from the **simplicity** and purity of devotion to Christ"* (see 2 Cor.11:2-4 NASB). Simple Prayer, therefore, is simply being in the presence of Jesus: no more, no less.

Come into the presence of the Lord *expecting* to meet with Him spirit-to-Spirit. Present your time as an offering to Him. Present yourself to Him and yield your will. Drop down to your spirit and open the door to your heart to welcome His Spirit. Seek God for Himself alone, and make relationship with Him your top priority!

Perhaps the way to describe *Simple Prayer* would be communing with God. We touch Him spirit-to-Spirit. Prayer is a relationship with a Person. The communion we experience in our time of prayer doesn't have to end as though we go in and out of prayer. We can learn to maintain our connection with the Lord throughout the day. It may take some effort at first to learn a new way of living but the reward of a life lived in peace is priceless.

When we practice the presence of God as a lifestyle, we begin to *abide* in Him. In John 15, Jesus tells us to abide in Him, using the metaphor of a branch connected to a vine. A branch must be attached to its life source to flourish and produce fruit.

Abide in Me, and I in you. As the branch cannot bear fruit of itself, unless it abides in the vine, neither can you, unless you abide in Me. "I am the vine, you are the branches. He who abides in Me, and I in him, bears much fruit; for without Me you can do nothing" (John 15:4-5).

Wait in God's presence. As you wait silently, without speaking, simply become aware of the presence of the Lord in your heart. This way of prayer is both a relationship with God and a discipline which encourages growth of the relationship. *Simple Prayer* is not intended to replace other types of prayer. However, it does bring deeper meaning to all prayer and leads you from more active kinds of prayer into prayer in which you wait in God's presence.

The two necessary ingredients of abiding prayer are silence and stillness. If you have ever stilled your thoughts in your prayer time or church to quietly enjoy God's presence, you have already experienced silent prayer. The mind does not become blank, but awareness of God increases.

GETTING STARTED

1. Decide on a time. My prayer time is: _____
   If you don't devote a specific prayer time into your schedule it is too easy to skip.

2. Choose a quiet place with a comfortable chair in which to sit. My quiet place is: _____

3. Get your Bible, a pen or pencil, and your journal so that you can keep a written record.

   ☐ Bible ☐ Pen ☐ Journal

4. How long should I spend in prayer? We suggest a minimum of 20 or 30 minutes at a time.

5. Try to pray through a cycle of at least 3 emotional healings a day.

6. If possible, ask someone to be your prayer partner.

SIMPLE PRAYER

Daily Prayer

In an attitude of prayer, silently focus on Christ within.

I. ***HONOR:*** *Start by presenting yourself to the Lord in humility and adoration as His servant. Honor God as a real person who is right there with you, not far away. Yield to His presence and desire God's will, His thoughts (revelation), and His emotions (the fruit of the Spirit).*

II. ***AWARENESS:*** *As you sense the presence of God, pay attention to the atmosphere. What facet of His nature is the Lord revealing to you? Love, comfort, peace, refreshing, holy anticipation? What words come to mind that describe the atmosphere? Pay attention to scriptures or pictures which corroborate what you feel. Don't just think about it, but receive, absorb, drink in. Allow it to be written on your heart. Later, take some action by writing it down, cherishing it, speaking of it, and living it!*

III. ***TIME:*** *How long should you spend in prayer? Enough time for your flesh to become still in the presence of God. How can you tell? Your thoughts will cease to wander, you will feel peace, and you will lose the urge to go do something other than pray (Psalm 131:2; Isaiah 40:31).*

IV. ***FIVE LOVING FUNCTIONS:*** *Your human spirit cooperates with the Holy Spirit in:*
   a. *Forgiving*
   b. *Loving*
   c. *Releasing (people and circumstances)*
   d. *Receiving*
   e. *Resisting*

CHAPTER 2

HEALING PRAYER

God desires to be Lord of our entire life, not just our "spiritual" life. Since God made us thinking, willing, feeling beings, He wants us to allow Him to rule over our thoughts, choices, and emotions.

- God's thoughts are higher than our thoughts (see Isa. 55:8-9; Rom. 11:33-34).
- God's will is preferable to the choices we would make on our own (see Prov. 3:5-7; 14:12).
- God's love is superior to our carnal emotions (see 1 Cor. 13; 1 John 2:15-17).

God is Spirit. The word "spirit" or "spirits" is used more than 900 times in the scriptures. In John 4:24, Jesus says that, "God is Spirit." Jesus also tells us that God is known and worshipped through the spirit. In other words, a spiritual God communicates and communes with man *in the spirit realm.*

God is spirit, and those who worship Him must worship in spirit and truth (John 4:24).

Flesh and spirit. Would you agree that you sometimes have *thoughts* and *emotions* that are clearly not godly? Do you occasionally make *choices* that are not God's will? The fallen nature of man, the flesh, is not at all like God's nature! They don't mix. Either flesh rules or spirit rules at any given time. When a person is saved, the spirit has been made alive, but the carnal nature wars against the spirit in them. Both the flesh and the spirit vie for control.

For the flesh lusts against the Spirit, and the Spirit against the flesh (Galatians 5:17).

Spirit-to-Spirit. A Christian connects with God spirit-to-Spirit by quieting the flesh and yielding to the Holy Spirit. This is what happens when you pray. To walk in the spirit, a believer must learn to maintain a spiritual connection with God in everyday life.

Surely I have calmed and quieted my SOUL, like a weaned child with his mother (Psalm 131:2).

If we live by the [Holy] Spirit, let us also walk by the Spirit. [If by the Holy Spirit we have our life in God, let us go forward walking in line, our conduct controlled by the Spirit] (Galatians 5:25 AMPC).

LOCATION

The number one principle of real estate is location, location, location. The first lesson to learn for effective Christian living is also location! It is essential to know the location of your spiritual real estate.

Locate Your Bible Heart. When the Bible talks about the heart, it is not referring to the chest area or physical heart. In the Old Testament and New Testament alike, words such as belly or bowels are regularly translated heart in English. In John 7:38, Jesus refers to the heart by the word *belly* in the Greek, *"He that believeth on me, as the scripture hath said, out of his BELLY shall flow rivers of living water."*

- The heart is the center of man's **inward** life and the sphere of **divine** influence.
- The Bible locates the heart in the **belly**, not the chest.

Locate your thoughts. This one should be easy! People always point to the head when you ask them the location of their thoughts.

Locate your emotions. The Bible tells us that the heart is below the chest, in the belly area, and is the seat of emotion. According to the Bible, the *emotional heart* is in the **belly**.

The words of a talebearer are as WOUNDS, and they go down into the innermost parts of the BELLY (Proverbs 18:8 KJV).

PRACTICE

Close your eyes and place your hand on your belly.

Think of a stressful situation in your life.

Now think of a pleasant memory.

Notice how it feels in your gut.

Locate your Will. The Bible tells us the belly or gut is not only the seat of our spirit and emotions, but also of our *conscience* and *will,* the faculties of choice and decision making. The word *will,* in some translations of the Old Testament, is translated *reins,* or literally our *kidneys.*

> *I the LORD search the heart, I try the REINS [kidneys], even to give every man according to his ways, and according to the fruit of his doings* (Jeremiah 17:10 KJV).

Locate the door of your heart. The door of the heart is the *will.* It is in the belly. Scripture tells us that the door of the heart can open or close. Jesus tells us, *"Behold, I stand at the DOOR and knock. If anyone hears My voice and opens the door, I will come in to him"* (Rev. 3:20).

YIELDING

One of the most powerful lessons followers of Jesus can learn is how to *yield* their will to God's will. Unless this lesson is learned, a believer will struggle in many areas of their Christian life.

Connect. Yielding instantly connects you to Christ within. When you *don't* yield, you are left to your own resources! When we yield and connect with God, God *works.*

> *It is God who is at work in you, both to will and to work for His good pleasure* (Philippians 2:13 NASB).

Distance is a deception. Christ is always with us. When we invite Him into our heart, He comes to dwell within us. He is our *Immanuel* which means, *"God with us"* (Matt. 1:23).

Drop down. *Drop down* is a shorthand term meaning "get out of your head and go to Christ in your heart." When we close our eyes and pray, we focus on Christ within. It's like dropping a bucket down in a well. When we acknowledge the Lord spirit-to-Spirit, we include Him in our life.

Counsel in the heart of man is like water in a deep well (Prov. 20:5 AMPC).

Peace is practical. Jesus is the Prince of Peace. When Jesus is ruling, His peace is present. As soon as you *drop down* and *yield* you feel His peace. The peace you feel in God's presence is available all the time. You don't have to be in your prayer closet to "drop down." Actually, you need peace even more when you are at work, on the road, or when the computer crashes.

[L]et the peace of God rule in your hearts (Colossians 3:15).

PRACTICE

Close your eyes and "drop down." Yield to Christ within. It is like relaxing, down low. It is the opposite of being tense. This opens the door of your heart, and makes space in your life for God. Yield even more. Jesus is the Prince of Peace. Sense the peace of being in His presence. Stay "dropped down" and open your eyes. As long as you drop down, you stay at peace—even with your eyes open!

God Emotions. In the Garden of Eden, before they sinned, Adam and Eve only experienced the love, joy, and peace of God—what we call God Emotions—in their emotions.

But the fruit of the Spirit is love, joy, peace, longsuffering, gentleness, goodness, faith, Meekness, temperance (Galatians 5:22-23 NASB).

When Adam sinned, his spirit was separated from God. He died a spiritual death. Harmony between God and man was fractured. Adam became flesh-ruled instead of spirit-ruled. Man's fallen nature and God's heavenly nature no longer matched. Adam's thoughts, choices, and emotions—in his soul—were now carnal, ruled by flesh. Adam and Eve felt toxic emotions for the first time.

Emotions are signals. When a believer yields to God, they experience God Emotions as the fruit of the Sspirit. When a Christian fails to yield, they experience carnal emotions. Your emotions sound the alarm to let you know which Kingdom is ruling. All negative emotions come from the enemy.

The fruit of the Spirit lets you know that the Prince of Peace is ruling in your heart. *Negative emotions* mean that the enemy has taken some ground. How do you know if you have entered Enemy Territory? Negative emotions. How do you know if you are in God's Territory? God Emotions, or the fruit of the Spirit!

> [T]he kingdom of God is…righteousness and peace and joy in the Holy Spirit (Romans 14:17.)

Forgiveness conveys us into God territory. Forgiveness is the God Tool that takes you out of Enemy Territory into God Territory. God rescued you from the kingdom of darkness and granted you citizenship in the kingdom of God.

> He [God] has delivered us from the power of darkness and conveyed us into the kingdom of the Son of His love (Colossians 1:13).

Negative emotions give the enemy legal ground to harass you. Forgiveness washes out toxic emotions and replaces them with supernatural peace…

NOTE: If you are a born again believer, it doesn't mean you have lost your *salvation* when you temporarily get in Enemy Territory, any more than a United States citizen loses their citizenship if they visit a foreign country.

FORGIVENESS

Christ the forgiver. Forgiveness is a Person. Christ is the forgiver so He forgives through us. We forgive by the grace of God. Christ Himself does the forgiving through us. *Christ the Forgiver* in us does all the work. And everything He does is easy for Him!

Grace is a Person. Have you learned the definition of "grace" as the *unmerited favor of God*? That is true. Grace is the personal presence of Christ empowering us *to be* and do all that He called us to be and all that He called us to do. But grace is much more than that. Grace is God doing for us what we can't do for ourselves.

Forgiveness defined. Forgiveness must be from the heart and include mind, will and emotions.

- Forgiveness is not optional; it is a command.
- Forgiveness releases us so that our lives won't be poisoned.
- Forgiveness releases others so that God can work in their lives.
- Forgiveness is canceling a debt.
- Forgiveness is ceasing to sit in the place of judgment and releasing others to God.

Forgiveness is NOT:

- Being a doormat.
- Pardoning in the sense of removing consequences.
- Just pretending to forget.
- Releasing someone from personal responsibility.

OPEN-FORGIVE-FRUIT

Receiving the gift of salvation. Remember when you got saved? What happened when you prayed, "Jesus, I ask you to save me and forgive me for my sins?" You *opened* the door of your heart to Jesus and received *forgiveness instantly* as a free gift. You then experienced *peace* with God. *"Behold, I stand at the door and knock. If anyone hears My voice and **opens the door**, I will come in..."* (Rev. 3:20).

*In Him we have redemption through His blood, the **forgiveness** of sins* (Ephesians 1:7).

*[T]here is **peace** with God through Jesus Christ* (Acts 10:36).

How did you RECEIVE Christ into your heart?
Open, forgiveness, fruit.

1. **OPEN.** You OPENED the door by YIELDING your will (Rev. 3:20).

2. **FORGIVENESS.** You experienced God's FORGIVENESS (Col. 1:13-14). Forgiveness removed the barrier which separated you from God.

3. **FRUIT.** You experienced PEACE *with* God by receiving forgiveness, experiencing the FRUIT of the Spirit (Rom. 5:1; Gal. 5:22-23).

Walking in the Spirit. How should you *live* the Christian life? You live the Christian life by walking in the Spirit. You can only "walk in the Spirit" when your spirit connects with God's Spirit. In John 15:5, Jesus says, *"I am the vine, you are the branches. He who abides in Me, and I in him, bears much fruit; for without Me you can do nothing."*

A believer walks in the Spirit by maintaining a spiritual connection with God, or *abiding* in Him. As soon as you disconnect, you are in the flesh. In the book of Colossians, Paul tells believers that the way they received salvation is the pattern for Christian living. *"As you..have received Christ Jesus the Lord, so walk in Him"* (Col. 2:6).

You began your life in Christ with the Spirit. Now do you try to complete it by your own power? That is foolish (Galatians 3:3 ERV).

How do you WALK in the Spirit?
Open, forgiveness, fruit.

1. **OPEN.** Keep the door OPEN by YIELDING your will (Rev. 3:20).

2. **FORGIVENESS.** Live a FORGIVENESS lifestyle. (Luke 24:46-47; Col. 3:12-13; 1 John 1:7). Forgiveness continually removes barriers separating you from God and others.

3. **FRUIT.** PEACE is evidence that you are right with God and people. Whenever you lose your PEACE, you can instantly regain it dropping down or forgiveness. You live in the peace *of* God (Phil. 4:9; Col. 3:15).

Deep Relief NOW

DRN PRAYER STEPS

FORGIVE IN THREE DIRECTIONS

Forgive God-Self-Others. Forgiveness goes in three directions: Toward God, self, and others. Sometimes we may need to forgive in two or more directions. If in doubt, forgive. You can't love or forgive too much!

1. ***God.*** God didn't do anything wrong, but people get angry at Him anyway. Sometimes people feel hurt that God didn't do what they wanted Him to do, or become angry that God didn't *stop* something from happening. Forgiving God gets *your* heart right by releasing your judgments toward him.

2. ***Self.*** If you are angry, disappointed with, or ashamed of yourself, you need to receive forgiveness for judging yourself so harshly. Frequently people are much harder on themselves than other people!

3. ***Others.*** Release forgiveness to other people. It sets *you* free!

PRACTICE

Forgiving

FIRST—First person or situation. *What is the first person or situation that comes to mind—in an image or memory?*

FEEL—Feel the feeling. *Allow yourself to feel. What is the emotion you feel in your gut?*

FORGIVE—Forgive. *Yield to Christ the Forgiver within and allow a river of forgiveness to flow from the belly until the emotion changes to peace.*

FACT—Fact. *After forgiving and getting peace, if there is a lie, renounce the lie out loud. Next, ask the Lord for the truth (scriptural fact) and receive it. (See chapter XXX)*

FILL—Fill. *(1) Forgive first, then (2) release demands on people to give you what you needed. (3) Receive filling from Christ within.*

NOTE: Most emotional healings require ONLY the first three steps.

Important keys for prayer. Christ is the forgiver so forgiveness works every time! Forgiveness is instant, not a process. There is no "big or little." It is all easy for Jesus! Sequence is important, so always go in God's order. Pray through one thing at a time until you get peace.

Forgiveness is the answer for dealing with conflict and offenses in the moment as well as the baggage of the past. God graciously cleans up a lot of things in a person's life at the moment of salvation and some ways of thinking, feeling, and motivation change immediately. However, sanctification is a *process*, and no one has dealt with every issue past and present.

Hurt people hurt people. When you are hurting, you will identify with the same hurts in others (trigger one another's wounds) or project your own issues on others. Hurt people overreact to even mild stimulation, lash out at others, withdraw from relationships, put up walls, see life through distorted lenses, and can be easily offended. Hurt people hurt people.

Healed people heal people. After the Lord brings healing to you, an anointing flows through the scar to bring healing to others. When you are healed, even the area where you were wounded the most can become your greatest anointing to minister life to the hurting. Healed people heal people!

CHAPTER 3

TAKING THOUGHTS CAPTIVE

We must take responsibility for our thoughts to walk in true freedom. The Bible instructs us to *"take captive every thought to make it obedient to Christ"* (2 Corinthians 10:5 NIV). How do we take thoughts captive and make them obedient to Christ in a practical way? We must begin by making two distinctions.

1. ***Make a distinction: The new creation.*** The real you is a new creation who loves God and loves His Word. The new creation always agrees with God. If a thought doesn't sound like something God would say, don't accept it.

   Therefore, if anyone is in Christ, he is a new creation; old things have passed away; behold, all things have become new (2 Corinthians 5:17).

2. ***Make a distinction: Inside or outside.*** We must differentiate between our own flesh and demonic influence.

   Check inside. When we feel something negative, we should first check inside, in our gut. We feel our emotions *inside* us. When we feel a negative emotion inside, we should deal with our emotions first through forgiveness until we feel peace.

   Check outside. When we have peace inside but feel *external* oppression, the pressure is outside us. When we have peace inside we have the spiritual authority and strength to resist anything negative in the atmosphere. If you accidently "own" a bad atmosphere outside of you, receive forgiveness and you will feel peace again.

   Therefore submit to God. Resist the devil and he will flee from you (James 4:7).

PRACTICE
Inside or Outside

Pay attention to how you feel in your gut right now. What is the feeling?

_____

_____

_____

Now pay attention to the atmosphere outside of you. How does it feel?

_____

_____

_____

TWO CATEGORIES OF THOUGHTS

Simple distractions. We give power to what we give attention to. When we lose our peace due to a mild distraction or fleeting worry, we should renounce it (silently or aloud).

- Release the thought into the hands of God until you feel peace again.
- When we "take a thought captive," we give it to God.

Repetitive thoughts. A repetitive thought with a corresponding negative emotion is a *mental stronghold.* If a lie comes in, it always comes in at the time of emotional wounding. (Most of the time, emotional wounds do *not* have a lie, or mental stronghold, attached to them.)

- When a lie *is* believed, it blocks the truth from being received.
- A lie becomes a repetitive thought we hear again and again but there is also a negative emotion attached.

Some examples of mental strongholds are:

- "I'm unworthy." What does God say?
- "I can't do anything right." What does God say?
- "I never belong." What does God say?
- "I'm a hopeless mess." What does God say?
- "I have to be in control." What does God say?

Is there a repetitive thought that bothers you from time to time? _____

_____

_____

_____

TESTING THOUGHTS

There are three tests we should apply to the thoughts we hear. If a thought is the wrong spirit, is unscriptural, or has bad fruit, don't tolerate the thought.

1. ***Test the thought by the Spirit.*** If the thought feels condemning, accusatory, or intrusive, it is not God.

2. ***Test the thought by the words.*** Does the thought agree with the Bible?

3. ***Test the thought by the fruit.*** Does it feel like the fruit of the Spirit? If we acted on the thought, what fruit would it produce?

PULLING DOWN STRONGHOLDS

To deal with a mental stronghold, always start with the emotion first through forgiveness.

- Without peace, we have no spiritual authority.
- When we *do* have peace, we have access to supernatural power that can defeat any lie.

PRACTICE

Start with Forgiveness

First. *What is the first person or situation that comes to mind—an image or memory?*

Feel. *Feel the feeling. Allow yourself to feel. What emotion do you feel in your gut when you picture that person or situation? (Every thought has a corresponding emotion.)*

Forgive. *Yield to Christ the forgiver within and allow a river of forgiveness to flow from the belly until the emotion changes to peace. If you are forgiving yourself, receive forgiveness from Christ in you. Allow forgiveness to flow out to others. If you are angry at or disappointed with God, forgive Him. If you are upset with yourself, yield and receive forgiveness from Christ within.*

Let truth be written on your heart. Once we have peace, the next step is to renounce the lie and let the Lord replace it with the truth. Truth comes up from our spirit in our heart and informs our mind. It becomes revelation which is written on the tablet of our heart.

PRACTICE

Remove Mental Strongholds

Fact. *After forgiving and getting peace, if there is a lie, renounce it out loud. Next, ask the Lord for the truth (scriptural fact) and receive it. (Lies always come in at the time of emotional wounding. When we forgive and get peace, we are in the place of power with the spiritual authority to dislodge the lie.)*

CHAPTER 4

FILLING EMOTIONAL NEEDS

During the prophet Jeremiah's day, if a source of fresh water such as a spring or river was not available, people would chisel out cisterns to catch rain water. A cistern is not a spring, a lake, or even a well. It is a not attached to any source of water. If it doesn't rain, you have no water. A *cracked* cistern is useless because any water collected leaks out.

In Jeremiah 2:13 God says that His people have committed two sins. First, they have forsaken God—the Fountain of living waters. Then they made for themselves broken cisterns that can't hold water—*substitutes* of their own making. That is a really bad trade! It is like trading a new Mercedes Benz for a junk yard car without an engine.

> *My people have committed two evils [sins]: they have forsaken Me, the Fountain of living waters, and they have hewn for themselves cisterns, broken [cracked] cisterns which cannot hold water* (Jeremiah 2:13 AMP).

Cisterns. God makes the fresh stream but man makes cisterns. Cisterns are limited but God's supply is endless. We try to fill the holes in our heart with substitutes that never quite satisfy. Even though we may know better, we still do it anyway. We involve ourselves with diversions, resources, entertainment, and projects trying to fill a void only Christ can fill. Substitutes include unhealthy relationships, food, shopping, drugs and alcohol, money, romance novels, hobbies, entertainment, and so forth.

Identifying Cisterns. People can easily identify a cistern in their lives when it is no longer available. Whenever someone panics, their cistern probably just broke! It was whatever they were relying on more than God. You could probably think of several things you feel like you "just can't do without." The easiest way to identify a cistern is to ask God to show you.

Dealing with Cisterns. To deal with a cistern, you need to make an exchange by disconnecting from the cistern and connecting to Christ the fountain. Any person, place, or thing that you choose instead of God is an idol. Substituting a cistern over God is idolatry.

When key elements are lacking in childhood, an individual may spend their entire life trying to meet emotional needs. Unfortunately, this pursuit is extremely damaging because people choose unhealthy ways of searching. Emotional neediness pushes other people away and robs us of the very happiness we are seeking. Most social and relational problems come from trying to meet our needs in the wrong way.

Legitimate emotional needs. God made us with legitimate emotional needs: love, trust, acceptance, belonging, affirmation, security, value, worth, and purpose. Ideally, parents should give their children good emotional foundations. However, many fall short of the ideal. Wounds suffered early in life can interfere with the stability of our emotional foundations.

Emotionally bankrupt parents have little emotional support to give to their children. They can't give something they themselves never received. If their own emotional needs are unmet, parents can't meet the emotional needs of their children. Nothing can ever fill a "black hole" in outer space. It just keeps absorbing more and more matter. Unmet needs in childhood result in *emotional black holes.* Individuals attempt to fill the inner cravings with counterfeits that never satisfy.

Filling Emotional Black Holes. Because people aren't perfect, God has made provision for healing and filling our needs. *"When my father and my mother forsake me, then the Lord will take care of me"* (Psa. 27:10). No matter what you've been through, God is able to heal you and provide what you needed.

PRACTICE

Filling Emotional Needs

If you have an emotional need that wasn't met (for example, love or approval), forgive the person(s) who should have met that need but didn't.

Apply the first-feel-forgive steps until you feel peace.

Fill. Allow God to fill the emotional need by releasing people who didn't meet the need into the hands of God from your gut until you no longer feel an inner demand concerning them.

When you have peace, welcome God into that area to fill the need.

CHAPTER 5

GUARDING YOUR WILL

[S]ubmit to God. Resist the devil and he will flee from you.—James 4:7

God has given us the ability to resist oppressive atmospheres and stay in peace. There is a proper way to resist the enemy and guard our heart. Although we can feel the atmosphere around us we can experience peace in our heart. We bear witness to outside pressure but don't take it in.

In a hostile environment or when you are in the presence of an angry person, drop down and let the peace of God guard your heart and your mind. Remember, we don't open our heart to the person; we open our heart to Christ in us. That way Jesus "stands" between us and any person who might confront us. Because Jesus is guarding us, we can resist attacks from both flesh and spirit.

AFTER OUR WILL

Both God and the devil are after our will. Why is our will so important? In the Garden of Eden, Adam's thoughts, choices, and emotions were in harmony with God's thoughts, will, and emotions. God's will is a flow of divine purpose. In heaven God's will is always perfectly expressed. He wants His will done on earth through yielded vessels. When we yield our will to God's will, we allow heaven to be released on earth through us.

Both God and the devil want our will so they can express their nature through us. Both God and the devil want our will so their plans and purposes will be accomplished on earth. God's nature is love and He wants to bring redemption to humankind. God has a divine plan for earth and He needs people to cooperate with Him. The devil's nature is fear and hate, and he wants to bring destruction and death to us. The devil has an evil plan for earth and he ensnares people to cooperate with him (see John 10:9-10).

Our behavior is determined by whatever controls our will. When a mother hears her child cry, she rushes to see what is wrong because her heart is moved by love and concern. Our will is motivated by emotions and thoughts, which are then expressed through our behavior. If our will is not engaged, we do nothing because we "don't want to." If we are thirsty, we choose to reach forth our hand and pick up a cup of water to drink. Our will has been "engaged" for action.

Consider the Gadarene demoniac. Jesus and His disciples crossed the Sea of Galilee and came to the region of Gadara. As soon as they got out of the boat they encountered a demon-possessed man who appeared wildly insane:

And when He had come out of the boat, immediately there met Him out of the tombs a man with an unclean spirit, who had his dwelling among the tombs; and no one could bind him, not even with chains, because he had often been bound with shackles and chains. And the chains had been pulled apart by him, and the shackles broken in pieces; neither could anyone tame him. And always, night and day, he was in the mountains and in the tombs, crying out and cutting himself with stones (Mark 5:2-5).

If the demon-possessed man was not manifesting his human nature, who was being expressed through him? The Scriptures tell us that evil spirits were expressing themselves through this man. When Jesus commanded the evil spirits to come out of him, they spoke and said they were "legion." In the time of Jesus, a legion made up an entire army of more than 5,000 soldiers.

God wants to work in and through His people on earth. He wants to connect with us, own us, and express His nature through us. When we live a yielded life, we are transformed more and more into the image of Christ. Peter reminds us:

But you are a chosen race, a royal priesthood, a dedicated nation, [God's] own purchased, special people, that you may set forth the wonderful deeds and display the virtues and perfections of Him Who called you out of darkness into His marvelous light (1 Peter 2:9 AMP).

God's Goal: Connect ☐ Own ☐ Express

The enemy also wants bodies in which to live. Evil spirits want to connect with us, own us, and express their nature through us. The devil wants to express his evil nature in thoughts, words, and actions. The Gadarene demoniac was demon-possessed. Evil spirits made a connection, owned his will, and began to express their personalities through him.

The Enemy's Goal: Connect ☐ Own ☐ Express

RESISTING THE ENEMY

To fight successfully against the enemy, we must make two distinctions. The first distinction is that the real you is a new creation. Start from the place of the new creation, fused together with Christ. Make a distinction between the new creation you and the thoughts and impressions that the enemy wants to impose on you. Say to yourself, "That's not the real me. The real 'me' is a new creation who loves God and loves His Word." The new creation you is *"more than a conqueror"* through Christ (see Rom. 8:37). We are already triumphant in Christ. Recognize that Christ has already won the victory over the enemy.

SELF-DELIVERANCE

We don't have to go to an "expert" for deliverance. Through Christ the deliverer within, we can do self-deliverance. When we submit to God and get peace inside, we have already won the victory. When we take back ground from the enemy, he has to flee from us. Self-deliverance involves three steps. First, get peace inside. In prayer, ask, "Where did this get started?" Forgive to wash out the negative emotion and you will feel peace. You have taken back legal ground which had been given to the enemy. Deliverance is usually automatic when the enemy has no ground.

Second, resist the outside atmosphere. The enemy can't get through a door you won't open. Yield to peace in your heart but resist the outside atmosphere. It is like having a spiritual screen door. You can feel the breeze, but mosquitoes can't come in. If you have peace inside and feel a bad atmosphere outside—such as depression, fear, or anger—don't take it in. If you give in to it by accident, receive forgiveness and get your peace back.

Third, guard your doors. The enemy tries to connect with you through two doors: the mind door or the emotion door. Remember, the enemy works from the outside to get your will. If you have peace, you are safe. Don't own all the thoughts that you hear in your head. If you hear a thought that doesn't sound like something God would say, don't accept it. It doesn't matter if the devil or your flesh says it, don't take it if God doesn't give it. When you have peace in your heart but still feel pressure, yield to Christ the deliverer in you and welcome Him to fill you from head to toe. As you yield to Him, allow His presence to radiate outwardly, pushing back anything oppressive in the atmosphere.

When we drop down and allow peace to guard our heart, we cultivate spiritual prowess, or strength and skill. You may fail at times, but what do you do when you fail? You forgive and receive forgiveness. Allow the forgiver to restore your peace. When we allow the Lord to rule our heart, we cultivate patience and hope.

As you practice the spiritual disciplines found in this journal, you will notice your spiritual strength increases. Things that once made you have a meltdown or greatly irritated you will eventually be slight annoyances that you easily release. Ever-increasing peace will become a way of life.

CHAPTER 6

DEALING WITH
SEXUAL ISSUES

For human beings, all sexual activity is spiritual. We are different from animals because we have spirits and are created in the image of God. For us, sex is therefore spiritual not just physical.

- Sex is an awesome force so powerful it can bring forth a *human life.*
- A loving marriage between one man and one woman provides (1) the mutual support and welfare of committed parents as well as (2) a stable home for raising children.
- Children can then be nurtured in love by both a father and mother who raise them in the *"training and instruction of the Lord"* (see Eph. 6:4 NIV).

Society as a whole recognized that sex should be reserved for marriage until the advent of the birth control pill. Sex was then unmoored from responsibility under God and cheapened to selfish entertainment. Because of the unique role of sex in God's creation, God gave instructions in the Bible to maintain the purity of the act to prevent defiling individuals, marriages, and future generations

- The guidelines and prohibitions in the Bible tell us how to avoid *demonic infestation* due to sexual sin.
- Sexual activity is "safe" only in a marriage between one man and woman.

*Therefore a man shall leave his father and mother and be joined to his wife, and they shall become **one flesh*** (Genesis 2:24).

*[F]rom the beginning of the creation, God 'made them male and female.' 'For this reason a man shall leave his father and mother and be joined to his wife, and **the two shall become one flesh**; so then they are no longer two, but one flesh. Therefore what God has joined together, let not man separate* (Mark 10:6-9).

Definition of Marriage. Marriage is *not* two people who are tennis buddies, partners in a business, a legal contract as in a "civil union." God defined marriage as a bodily, emotional, and spiritual covenant between a man and a woman. The Lord Himself performed the first marriage ceremony between Adam and Eve (see Gen. 2:22-24).

Who gave the definition of the word "marriage"? _____

Do humans have a right to change it? _____

GOD'S PURPOSE FOR MARRIAGE

1. Marriage was established by God to give joy and satisfaction to human-kind.

Now the Lord God said, "It is not good (sufficient, satisfactory) that the man should be alone; I will make him a helper (suitable, adapted, complementary) for him" (Genesis 2:18 AMP).

2. Christian marriages are designed to reflect unity in the Godhead.

Then God said, "Let us make man in our image, in our likeness...." So, God created man in his own image, in the image of God he created him; male and female he created them (Genesis 1:26-27).

3. Marriage was designed to continue and increase the human race by producing godly children who are raised in stable, loving families. *God blessed them and said to them, "Be fruitful* [and] *multiply"* (Gen. 1:28).

4. The family is the building block of human society. The parent's marriage is designed to model healthy social relationships for their children. Healthy families form healthy communities.

SEXUAL SIN

Demons do not mold to all fleshly manifestations, inner wounds, or sins, but sexual sins automatically give legal ground to demons. Sexual sin gives seducing spirits permission to infest a person's life.

- Seducing spirits can link to unclean emotional attachments even when there has been no physical contact. (It doesn't matter if there hasn't been actual physical involvement.)
- The King James Version of the Bible terms this type of lust inordinate affection, or "desire with a twist."

Soul Ties. The term "soul tie" is usually applied to an impure emotional connection with seducing spirits involved. However, there are both clean and unclean emotional attachments. In the Bible, David and Jonathan had a healthy emotional connection (see 1 Sam. 18:1-3).

An unclean soul tie does not disappear over time. Soul ties are not always romantic attachments. Parents can develop soul ties with their own children. Patients or clients sometimes form soul ties with counselors or physicians. Co-dependent relationships are based on soul ties.

Why do you think David and Jonathan's relationship was healthy?

_____

_____

_____

_____

What would make a relationship unhealthy?

_____

_____

_____

_____

Spiritual Adultery. If a married person develops an emotional attraction with some person other than a spouse, they are committing spiritual adultery.

Emotional attachments between co-workers are so common in the business world that the expression "work spouse" has been coined. According to a recent survey, 23% of all employees reported that they had a work spouse.[1]

If spiritual adultery is not dealt with, it usually leads to physical adultery. Believers must continue to be vigilant after breaking a soul tie because the other party will usually attempt to re-establish the connection.

> *You have heard that it was said to those of old, "You shall not commit adultery." But I say to you that whoever looks at a woman to lust for her has already committed adultery with her in his heart* (Matthew 5:27-28).

> *Whoever commits adultery with a woman lacks understanding; He... destroys his own soul* (Proverbs 6:32).

Why would spiritual adultery progress to physical adultery? _____

_____

_____

_____

Why would someone attempt to re-establish the connection after a soul tie is broken?

_____

_____

_____

_____

Seducing Spirits. Individuals under the influence of seducing spirits lose their ability to make logical decisions. They get what we call "the stupids," failing to see what everyone around them clearly understands. They get defensive and angry if someone disagrees with them.

> *[T]he path of the just is like the shining sun, that shines ever brighter unto the perfect day. The way of the wicked is like darkness; they do not know what makes them stumble* (Proverbs 4:18-19).

PRACTICE

Dealing with Seducing Spirits

In sexual sin or when we are sinned against, there may be a variety of emotions that surface including arousal, guilt, shame, disgust, fear, and so forth. Sometimes there is anger toward someone who failed to provide protection or toward God if we blame Him. "Why did God allow that to happen to me?" Often a person blames themselves even if they were clearly victimized. Both real and imagined guilt are resolved the same way—by receiving forgiveness.

Pray: In an attitude of prayer, pray in order as people or events come to mind.

Feel the feeling: Dealing with the titillation or arousal specifically is necessary for dealing with the seducing spirit. If you just feel guilt and shame, deal with that first, then allow yourself to feel the arousal.

Forgive: Forgive God, self, and others. Receive forgiveness and cleansing for yourself. Pray through emotional wounds, such as hurt or fear. Sometimes different emotions must be prayed through individually. For example, there is usually titillation or arousal, guilt, and shame.

Receive cleansing: Receive forgiveness and cleansing from Christ within. Allow the Lord to wash and cleanse your spirit. Your head will remember, but your spirit can forget.

Break soul ties: Break soul tie(s) as an act of your will and give your emotions back to God. In the case of pornography, soul ties in fantasy relationships need to be broken. Usually demonic activity leaves automatically, but it can be rebuked if necessary.

Warfare Strategy. When we are not entangled with unhealthy soul ties, God can draw us together in healthy relationships through divine appointments, divine connections, divine order, and divine purpose. God wants to deliver us from unclean entanglements so He can accomplish His purposes through the church. The Lord desires to set us free from ungodly soul ties so He can connect right relationships in the right way—with the bond of peace.

[K]eep the unity of the Spirit in the bond of peace (Ephesians 4:3).

ENDNOTE

1. E. Patrick, "Seven signs you have a work spouse," CNN.com/living, November 10, 2008. (June 2, 2010); http://www.cnn.com/2008/LIVING/worklife/11/10/cb.seven .signs.work.spouse/ accessed March 10, 2015.

SECTION TWO

DAYS 1–8

Honoring God as a Person

Day One
God with You

I. HONORING GOD AS A PERSON

I am the vine, you are the branches. He who abides in Me, and I in him, bears much fruit; for without Me you can do nothing.—John 15:5

[T]hose who honor Me I will honor.—1 Samuel 2:30

Daily Prayer

Now you are ready to begin. Each day when you come into the presence God, start by honoring Him. Pray along with the ***Daily Prayer*** CD. Start by getting into an attitude of prayer. Close your eyes and place your hand on your belly area, your spirit man, to help you focus on Christ within your heart.

- Honor God as a real Person who is with you.
- Relax and listen to the *Daily Prayer* CD.
- Ignore distracting thoughts and just keep returning your focus to Christ within.
- If you think of something important that you need to remember later, make a note and return to prayer.
- Write down any impressions or scripture verses that come to mind.

_____

_____

_____

_____

_____

_____

_____
_____
_____
_____

Healing Prayer

Pray along with the *Healing Prayer* CD. **The *Healing Prayer* CD is your personal trainer for heart cleansing.** The Lord knows all about you and He wants to set you free from troubled areas hidden in your heart. Many times the conscious mind forgets all about hurts and fears but they still affect our lives even if they are under the surface.

- Allow the Lord to reveal anything He wants, allowing forgiveness to bring healing.
- Keep a brief record of what you pray about and what the Lord reveals to you.
- Pray in the order that things come to mind, and write down revelation that you get.
- During this Challenge try to deal primarily with as much baggage from the past as you can.
- Try to pray through at least <u>three</u> issues every day.

_____
_____
_____
_____
_____
_____
_____
_____
_____

Day Two
Harmony with God

[D]o not be conformed to this world, but be transformed by the renewing of your mind [Gk. nous—mind, will, emotions], that you may prove what is that good and acceptable and perfect will of God.—Romans 12:2

For as the heavens are higher than the earth, so are My ways higher than your ways, and My thoughts than your thoughts.—Isaiah 55:9

Daily Prayer

Pray along with the ***Daily Prayer*** CD. *"Lord, I want to touch you in prayer this morning. Knit my heart with Your heart in the reality of Your presence."* You are a thinking, willing, feeling being and you were created by God to be in perfect harmony with Him—His thoughts, His choices, and His emotions.

- Prayer brings you into alignment with the heart of God, to change *you.*
- Allow the Lord to reveal His thoughts to your heart, adjust your choices, and unite you with His love.

Healing Prayer

Pray along with the *Healing Prayer* CD. Deal with any issue that comes to mind, even if you think it is seem small and insignificant. Come into the presence of the Lord just like a child who runs to the embrace of a loving parent.

- Invite the Lord to search your heart. Let forgiveness wash away pain.
- Write down a brief description of issues that come up, and note changes in perception after forgiveness.

_____

_____

_____

_____

_____

_____

_____

_____

_____

_____

_____

_____

_____

_____

_____

_____

_____

_____

_____

Day Three
Christ Within

*God willed to make known what are the riches of the glory of this mystery among the Gentiles: which is **Christ in you, the hope of glory***.
—Colossians 1:27

Daily Prayer

Pray along with the ***Daily Prayer*** CD. Make room for God to rise up within you, over your mind, will, emotions. Many believers don't have a clear understanding about who they are in Christ and how very near He is. God dwells in heaven, but He also dwells in your heart. God is with you. His glory is within you. You do not have to beg Him for His presence, all you have to do is yield to Him.

_____

_____

_____

_____

_____

_____

_____

_____

_____

_____

_____

_____

_____

_____

_____

Healing Prayer

Pray along with the *Healing Prayer* CD. You are coming to offer yourself to the Lord. He sees you as a New Creation, which is your real identity. God desires to reveal Himself to you and for you to glimpse the glorious treasure hid in your heart in Him. Cleansing and healing the heart remove barriers that prevent you from knowing Him more fully and from knowing who you really are in Christ.

- Enjoy God's love even in the process of sanctification.
- Allow the Lord to soften your heart and increase your sensitivity.
- Pray through a cycle of the people and situations that the Lord brings to mind.

Day Four
Communion and Intimacy

The Spirit Himself bears witness with our spirit that we are children of God.—Romans 8:16

God is Spirit, and those who worship Him must worship in spirit and truth.—John 4:24

Daily Prayer

Pray along with the **Daily Prayer** CD. When we are born again our spirits can commune with God but the carnal mind, will, and emotions (soul) cannot know God. Because the fallen nature, the soul of man, is not at all like God's nature, we can commune with God only by the spirit. Therefore, man must quiet the soul and surrender to the Holy Spirit to be in communion with God. When you yield to the will to God, your spirit touches God, and the spirit takes authority over your soul. Yield to Christ within and welcome His presence to touch every area of your life. Welcome Him to strengthen you in your innermost being, to flow through your mind, will, and emotions.

_____

_____

_____

_____

_____

_____

_____

_____

_____

_____

Healing Prayer

Pray along with the *Healing Prayer* CD. Do not become frustrated if something interferes with your prayer time, such as a phone call or doorbell ringing. Simply persevere and return to prayer as soon as you can. If you oversleep or feel upset with yourself, receive forgiveness. You heavenly Father is delighted that you are drawing closer to Him. He does not expect perfection and neither should you.

- It brings pleasure to God's heart every time you set aside time to commune with Him.
- Do not fight runaway thoughts. Just ignore them while you keep returning your attention to Christ within.

Day Five
Making Space for God

We love Him because He first loved us.—1 John 4:19

He chose us in Him before the foundation of the world, that we should be holy and without blame before Him in love.—Ephesians 1:4

Daily Prayer

Pray along with the **Daily Prayer** CD. Enjoy God's presence whether or not anything "happens." Being with God is more important than anything else. Just love Him and receive His love. Jesus has been eager for you to come be with Him so He can offer you His love. When you give Him your time and wait before Him, you are making space for Him.

Healing Prayer

Pray along with the ***Healing Prayer*** CD. Pray along with the Healing Prayer CD as it leads you through the steps for healing the heart. Present yourself to the Lord. *"Lord, cleanse me of anything interfering with our relationship!"*

- When you present your heart to the Lord, pray according to *His* order.
- God knows how everything is connected and how you should pray.
- Deal with as much baggage from the past as possible.

_____

_____

_____

_____

_____

_____

_____

_____

_____

_____

_____

_____

_____

_____

_____

_____

_____

_____

_____

Day Six
Dealing with Distractions

The grace of the Lord Jesus Christ, and the love of God, and the communion of the Holy Spirit be with you all.—2 Corinthians 13:14

Daily Prayer

Pray along with the ***Daily Prayer*** CD. In His presence is fullness of joy (Psalm 16:11). If you have difficulty with distracting thoughts or circumstances that interrupt your communion with the Lord, do not become frustrated with yourself. Write them down and simply melt back into God's presence. Rejoice in spite of everyday trials and the troublesome situations of life. When you continue to release it all back to the Lord, He will make everything turn out for good by His love and grace. This is really what trusting God is all about.

Healing Prayer

Pray along with the *Healing Prayer* CD. It helps you keep your focus on Christ within if you keep your hand on your belly as a reminder. *"Lord, you may go anywhere in my heart. You are welcome to go anywhere you want. I give you permission you to search my heart right now."*

- Remember to go in order. Don't skip or ignore issues.
- Pray through each memory one at a time until you get peace.
- As soon as you get peace go on to the next person or situation that comes to mind.
- When you have prayed through a cycle there will be a perception of completion, or sense of rest.

_____

_____

_____

_____

_____

_____

_____

_____

_____

_____

_____

_____

_____

_____

_____

_____

_____

_____

Day Seven
The Goodness of God

Men shall speak of the might of Your awesome acts, and I will declare Your greatness. They shall utter the memory of Your great goodness, and shall sing of Your righteousness. The LORD is gracious and full of compassion, slow to anger and great in mercy.—Psalm 145:6-8

Daily Prayer

Pray along with the **Daily Prayer** CD. Reflect on the goodness of God as you commune with Him. Focus on Christ in you. Notice that when you are aware of loving God you experience a sense of gratitude. This is true praise from the heart. As you continue yielding to God's love, often the sense of peace that you feel in His presence begins to change to joy. That is the joy of the Lord. You are being strengthened by the Holy Spirit (see Isaiah 40:31).

_____

_____

_____

_____

_____

_____

_____

_____

_____

_____

_____

_____

Healing Prayer

Pray along with the ***Healing Prayer*** CD. You are coming to offer yourself fully to the Lord without analysis, restriction, or censoring. You are surrendering yourself to your Lord. He is more than willing and able to restore whatever was withheld or taken from you (Joel 2:25).

- Allow the Lord to show you areas where childish delight was stolen.
- Forgive, release demands, and then allow the Lord to fill those areas.

Review of Week One

PRAYER PARTNER: If you have not yet done so, you may want to ask someone (a friend or your spouse) to be your prayer partner for healing prayer. It is helpful to be mutually accountable. Be sure to keep it confidential! If you can't pray together in person, prayer over the phone can be very effective. Give one another permission to not name names or give details.

My prayer partner is _____

1. What are the main thoughts that the Lord has been speaking to your heart? List a few of them here.

2. Write one or two scriptures that have spoken to your heart. Why?

3. What difficulties have you overcome? Which area has been the most problematic for you this week?

   - Mind
   - Will
   - Emotions

4. What theme(s) have you noticed in your emotional healings? For example, rejection, betrayals, disappointment, etc.

5. What lies (if any) have been replaced by the truth? Make a list.

LIE	TRUTH

NOTES

_____

_____

_____

_____

_____

_____

_____

_____

_____

_____

_____

_____

_____

_____

_____

_____

_____

_____

_____

_____

_____

_____

_____

_____

_____

_____

_____

_____

_____

Day Eight
Learning to Abide

[A]bide in My love.—John 15:9

Daily Prayer

Pray along with the **Daily Prayer** CD. True fruitfulness comes only from intimacy. Too many believers rely on their own resourcefulness rather than inquiring of God and relying on His power to accomplish. The ultimate goal in honoring God is to learn to abide in Him, connected at the heart, spirit-to-Spirit, breath to breath. When we are in peace, we are abiding. Deal quickly with anything that causes you to lose your peace during the day.

_____

_____

_____

_____

_____

_____

_____

_____

_____

_____

_____

_____

_____

_____

_____

_____

_____

Healing Prayer

Pray along with the *Healing Prayer* CD. Are there some areas of your life with which you are frustrated even though you have tried to change? If you have been unsuccessful in accomplishing something in your life and you are angry at yourself, then you haven't been trusting the Lord to do the changing. Ask the Lord to show you the root(s) and let Him deal with it. Then God's life can flow through your life. A branch on a vine simply allows life to flow through it.

- Allow the Lord to soften your heart and increase your sensitivity.
- When the Lord shows you that you have an inner demand for something, release it back into His hands. Let it go. He wants to have first place in your life.

_____

_____

_____

_____

_____

_____

_____

_____

_____

_____

_____

_____

_____

_____

_____

_____

SECTION THREE

DAYS 9–12

Listening (Awareness)

Day Nine
Increased Sensitivity

II. LISTENING (Awareness)

Then they brought little children to Him, that He might touch them.
—Mark 10:13

[Y]ou will seek Me and find Me, when you search for Me with all your heart.—Jeremiah 29:13

Daily Prayer

Pray along with the ***Daily Prayer*** CD. Learn greater sensitivity in prayer to encounter God in TOUCH. Pay attention to the whispers of the Spirit. When you come before the Lord in prayer and become quiet, pay attention to the atmosphere in the room where you are praying. How would you describe it? Does it feel peaceful, like an embrace, sweetly affectionate, or safe and secure? As you pay attention to the atmosphere, note any descriptive words that come to mind. Write them down.

_____

_____

_____

_____

_____

_____

_____

_____

_____

_____

Healing Prayer

Pray along with the *Healing Prayer* CD. It is particularly important to deal with childhood issues about parents. Wounds from parents have a tremendous influence in forming the foundations of our lives. Often people will just see a parent's face, but it is vital to deal with the specific memories that come to the surface. When you have emotional overreactions during the day, ask the Lord to show you where that got started in your life so that the root can be removed.

- Ask the Lord to show you memories of your father.
- If you feel a *wall of resistance*, the wall is your will. Allow forgiveness to flow through and remove the wall. (A wall is a defense mechanism of self-protection, based in fear.)
- If you forgive but still feel an ache inside (for love, attention, approval) then release demands on him to meet that need, and drink in the love of God to fill the hole.

_____

_____

_____

_____

_____

_____

_____

_____

_____

_____

_____

_____

_____

_____

_____

_____

Day Ten
Absorb and Cherish

[Martha] had a sister called Mary, who also sat at Jesus' feet and heard His word . . . "Mary has chosen that good part, which will not be taken away from her."—Luke 10:39, 42

Pray along with the ***Daily Prayer*** CD. If the Lord shows you something or you get a word or verse, write it down while never leaving the precious union in the Spirit. Hold that word close to your heart, cherish is as heavenly treasure of priceless value. Absorb it, hold it in the anointing. Allow it to grow. The Lord is your Master; you are the student. As long as you remain at His feet, He will continue to reveal Himself to you.

Daily Prayer

Does a scripture verse come to mind? As you wait silently, stay focused on the Lord and notice that the anointing increases while you meditate on the verse. Write down any additional impressions or words, but do not let your attention wander from the Lord Himself. In other words, don't start analyze mentally or begin researching in books, dictionaries, or commentaries, but just enjoy Him.

_____

_____

_____

_____

_____

_____

_____

_____

_____

Healing Prayer

Pray along with the *Healing Prayer* CD. Pray through issues concerning your mother. Allow the nurture of the Lord to fill in places that didn't receive the love that you needed as a child. Some wounds were just painful, but this type of healing restores the damaged foundations of our lives.

- The Lord says He will care for us and give us what we needed even if we were forsaken by mother and father.
- Once again, it is necessary to forgive, release demands, then receive filling.

Day Eleven
Heavenly Treasure

But we have this treasure in earthen vessels, that the excellence of the power may be of God and not of us.—2 Corinthians 4:7

Daily Prayer

Pray along with the **Daily Prayer** CD. You are indwelt by God! The God of the universe has chosen to reside inside you. *"In Him we live, and move, and have our being"* (Acts 17:28). So what is left for you to do other than to rest as He works in you and through you? You were a pauper, and He has filled you with the riches of heaven. Allow gratitude to arise in your heart, that God has blessed you with a great inheritance. He has lifted you up and made you a joint-heir with His very own Son.

_____

_____

_____

_____

_____

_____

_____

_____

_____

_____

_____

_____

_____

_____

_____

Healing Prayer

Pray along with the ***Healing Prayer*** CD. Pray through areas where you have felt disappointed in your life. You don't have to understand, but you must give up the internal demand for a do-over based on your own understanding.

- Forgive people, forgive God, forgive yourself, and release situations back into God's hands.
- Receive forgiveness for insisting that God answer to you, rather than you being a servant to Him.

_____

_____

_____

_____

_____

_____

_____

_____

_____

_____

_____

_____

_____

_____

_____

_____

_____

_____

_____

_____

Day Twelve
Shalom Shalom

You will guard him and keep him in perfect and constant peace whose mind [both its inclination and its character] is stayed on You, because he commits himself to You, leans on You, and hopes confidently in You.—Isaiah 26:3 AMP

Daily Prayer

Pray along with the **Daily Prayer** CD. Position yourself in awareness, touching spirit to spirit. Remain in the Presence of God until you experience His PEACE in your whole being: mind, will, emotions are quieted. You cannot trust God and be anxious or stressed at the same time. How do we trust God in everyday life? One Old Testament definition of *trust* is "to make someone your refuge." Prayer should not be something that you leave behind when you leave your prayer closet. Prayer is a Person who is always with you. All you have to do is open your heart to Him and you are instantly trusting in Him. If you begin to feel anxious, yield to Him and His peace will immediately return.

Healing Prayer

Pray along with the ***Healing Prayer*** CD. While you are in prayer, ask the Lord to reveal any areas of your life which you need to surrender more completely to Him. Pray through these areas one at a time, releasing each into the hands of a loving, capable God. If you feel any internal resistance you may need to face any fears, or strings, that are attached. Do not be afraid to face your fears head on, and be bold to release right through concerns and worries. This is a work of the Cross, because you are choosing God over your fleshly insecurities.

- Ask the Lord to show you situations from your childhood that are interfering with your ability to trust God and pray them through.
- When you have forgiven, released, and have peace ask the Lord to speak a scripture verse. Drink it in and allow it to deepen while you stay there awhile and enjoy being with Him.

SECTION FOUR

DAYS 13–38
Time

Day Thirteen
Deeper Still

III. TIME

Deep calls unto deep at the noise of Your waterfalls; All Your waves and billows have gone over me. The LORD will command His lovingkindness in the daytime, and in the night His song shall be with me—A prayer to the God of my life.—Psalm 42:7-8

Daily Prayer

Pray along with the ***Daily Prayer*** CD. We recommend spending at least 20 to 30 minutes in prayer. Others suggest a minimum of 20 minutes *twice a day*. Let the Lord lead you and show you how He wants you to schedule time with Him. Allow yourself to stay a little longer in your time of prayer today. Quietness has settled…allow deep tranquility to envelope your heart, and let the Holy Spirit take you deeper still.

Healing Prayer

Pray along with the *Healing Prayer* CD. Welcome the Lord to go into every area of your life, past, present, and future. As you give Him time, allow His presence to saturate your heart.

- Ask the Lord to show you any areas in which He wants you to surrender more fully to Him.
- Release these areas to Him and notice how your awareness of His presence increases.

Day Fourteen
Yielding Increases Peace

Surely I have calmed and quieted my soul, like a weaned child with his mother; Like a weaned child is my soul within me.—Psalm 131:2

Daily Prayer

Pray along with the ***Daily Prayer*** CD. Enjoy where you are now, then practice yielding even more, and you will notice that the peace increases. Quietness has settled. Allow deep tranquility to envelope your heart, and let the Holy Spirit take you deeper still.

- If you feel any impressions or increase in God's presence, pay attention to how it feels in the atmosphere, and write down any words that come to mind, such as *comforting, sweet, tender,* and so forth.
- The impressions you sense are the whispers of the Spirit.

_____

_____

_____

_____

_____

_____

_____

_____

_____

_____

_____

_____

_____

Healing Prayer

Pray along with the *Healing Prayer* CD. Welcome the Lord to go into every area of your life. As you give Him time, allow His presence to saturate your heart.

- Welcome the Lord to search all areas of your heart. If you feel resistance anywhere, simply agree with Him, yield, and He will melt away barriers
- Every time a barrier is removed, your sensitivity increases.

_____

_____

_____

_____

_____

_____

_____

_____

_____

_____

_____

_____

_____

_____

_____

_____

_____

_____

_____

_____

Review of Week Two

1. What are the main thoughts the Lord has been speaking to your heart?

2. What impressions have you noticed in the atmosphere?

3. Write one or two of the scriptures that stand out. Why?

4. What theme(s) have you noticed in your emotional healings this past week?

5. Have you been practicing staying in peace in your daily activities? When you lose your peace, deal with it quickly through forgiveness and/or release and you will quickly return to peace. NOTE: This is the main thing that you should practice in everyday life during the Challenge.

6. Don't expect perfection or become disappointed in yourself. Rejoice in every baby step of progress!

Thought for the Week

What counts is whether we have been transformed into a new creation. May God's peace and mercy be upon all who live by this principle; they are the new people of God.—Galatians 6:15-16 NLT

Only the Lord can bring transformation. You are being transformed into your New Creation identity, the real you. Each area of your life that is touched by God increases your anointing. An increased anointing allows you to release more of God to others.

Day Fifteen
God-Protected

*God's **peace** [shall be yours, that tranquil state of a soul assured of its salvation through Christ, and so fearing nothing from God and being content with its earthly lot of whatever sort that is, that peace] which transcends all understanding shall garrison and mount guard over your hearts and minds in Christ Jesus.*—Philippians 4:7 AMP

Daily Prayer

Pray along with the ***Daily Prayer*** CD. Enjoy the sweet touch of God's Spirit not only in you, but as this touching increases, you feel God's PEACE guarding (garrisoning as a fortress) your heart and mind through Christ Jesus. Notice that your heart feels tranquil, and thoughts do not distract you or cause you to lose your peace.

_____

_____

_____

_____

_____

_____

_____

_____

_____

_____

_____

_____

_____

_____

Healing Prayer

Pray along with the *Healing Prayer* CD. Welcome the Lord to deal with hidden root areas that are connected to any current loss of peace showing up with the people and circumstances of your daily life.

- Pray through at least one complete cycle.
- Don't dismiss anything that comes to mind as trivial or unimportant, but go ahead and deal with it.

_____

_____

_____

_____

_____

_____

_____

_____

_____

_____

_____

_____

_____

_____

_____

_____

_____

_____

_____

Day Sixteen
Surrounded by God

I will say of the LORD, "He is my refuge and my fortress; My God, in Him I will trust." He shall cover you with His feathers, and under His wings you shall take refuge; His truth shall be your shield and buckler.—Psalm 91:2, 4

The heavens and earth will shake; but the LORD will be a shelter for His people.—Joel 3:16

Daily Prayer

Pray along with the ***Daily Prayer*** CD. Experience God touching you within as well as being encompassed all about by His Presence—a canopy of God's Presence. God Himself is your shelter, your armor, your protection.

- The enemy can't touch the fruit of the Spirit. As long as you are in peace, you are surrounded with God's protection.
- Allow God to teach you to wear the full armor of God, and walk in shoes of peace (Ephesians 6:15).

_____

_____

_____

Healing Prayer

Pray along with the *Healing Prayer* CD. Allow the Lord to show you areas where you feel insecure and release them back into the hands of God. Fear and anxiety rob you of the ability to feel safe and secure in God.

- Invite God to search your heart for roots of fear.
- Perfect love casts out fear.

_____

_____

_____

_____

_____

_____

_____

_____

_____

_____

_____

_____

_____

_____

_____

Day Seventeen
Saturated by God

[T]o know the love of Christ which surpasses knowledge, that you may be filled up to all the fullness of God.—Ephesians 3:19 NASB

Daily Prayer

Pray along with the ***Daily Prayer*** CD. Experience God filling and saturating your entire being with His goodness. Welcome Him into every fiber of your being spirit, soul, and body. Invite the Holy Spirit to touch and strengthen your spirit and flow through your thoughts, choices, and emotions. Welcome the Lord into all areas of your life, including finances and relationships. Finally, welcome His healing anointing into your physical body.

Healing Prayer

Pray along with the *Healing Prayer* CD. Your mind, will, and emotions are like the sails of a sailboat. When the wind blows and the sails are set properly, the wind moves the vessel. There is always a wind of some sort filling your sails, but it is either the wind of flesh or the Holy Spirit. Welcome the wind of God into your thoughts and allow Him to deal unscriptural thinking. Invite Him into your choices to realign you with His will, and into your emotions to experience His peace.

- Allow God to deal with the roots of negative thoughts, choices, and emotional pain.
- Present yourself and your life back to God, as a love offering to Him.

Day Eighteen
Covered by God's Love

*My people will live in peaceful dwelling places, in secure homes, in undisturbed places of rest—*Isaiah 32:18

*Yes, I have loved you with an everlasting love; Therefore with lovingkindness I have drawn you—*Jeremiah 31:3

Daily Prayer

Pray along with the ***Daily Prayer*** CD. Feel PEACE deepening and the weight surrounding and covering you—a mantle of God's love wrapping around you. Rest in Him as you cherish and absorb His love for you. Welcome the love of God to fill you in every area.

Healing Prayer

Pray along with the *Healing Prayer* CD. Cleansing and healing the heart remove barriers that prevent you from knowing God's love more completely. God loved you even before the foundations of the earth were formed. He loved you and carried you in His heart for æons and æons of time in eternity past. God loved you before you could ever love Him back or do anything to try to earn His approval. Don't work for His love, just accept it and allow Him to embrace you.

- Enjoy the love of God even in the process of sanctification. His love for you makes transformation possible.
- God knows where He is taking you and how to get you there, and He never expects you to be perfect. He can even fix your mistakes.
- Receive forgiveness for yourself and melt into His love.

Day Nineteen
Stillness

And behold, the Lord passed by, and a great and strong wind rent the mountains and broke in pieces the rocks before the Lord, but the Lord was not in the wind; and after the wind an earthquake, but the Lord was not in the earthquake; And after the earthquake a fire, but the Lord was not in the fire; and after the fire [a sound of gentle stillness and] a still, small voice.—1 Kings 19:11-12 AMP

Daily Prayer

Pray along with the ***Daily Prayer*** CD. Come into the presence of God today and wait with a quiet and expectant heart. As you wait quietly and wait before the Lord, allow the sense of communion with Him to grow and increase. Experience stillness within and stillness without. You are now drawing from another kind of life, a heavenly life source, with a heavenly language that can only be heard in gentle stillness, a still small voice.

_____

_____

_____

_____

_____

_____

_____

_____

_____

_____

_____

Healing Prayer

Pray along with the ***Healing Prayer*** CD. Healing prayer removes obstacles in your life so that you can continue to bring the sense of that higher life into the mundane activities of daily living. Anything that robs you of your peace during the day can instantly be removed by forgiveness.

- Any root issues revealed and dealt with in your time of healing prayer will allow God to fill more of your heart.
- As God fills more of your heart, you will notice an increase in the peace of His presence all day long.

Day Twenty
Strengthened by God

[T]hose who wait on the LORD shall renew their strength; They shall mount up with wings like eagles, they shall run and not be weary, they shall walk and not faint.—Isaiah 40:31

Daily Prayer

Pray along with the *Daily Prayer* CD. Whenever your spirit encounters God, you receive spiritual strength from Him. Sense the security, safety, and all sufficiency that comes from Him.

_____

_____

_____

_____

_____

_____

_____

_____

_____

_____

_____

_____

_____

_____

_____

_____

Healing Prayer

Pray along with the *Healing Prayer* CD. Welcome the Lord to search all areas of your life, past, present, and future. As He heals your heart, allow His strength to fill you.

- Pray through roots of weakness and failure in your life.
- Forgive God, self, and others.
- Release yourself from over responsibility, and place yourself in God's hands.
- Exchange your feeble ability and receive God's power.

_____

_____

_____

_____

_____

_____

_____

_____

_____

_____

_____

_____

_____

_____

_____

_____

_____

_____

_____

Day Twenty-One
The All Sufficient God

How precious is Your lovingkindness, O God! And the children of men take refuge in the shadow of Your wings. They drink their fill of the abundance of Your house; and You give them to drink of the river of Your delights. For with You is the fountain of life; In Your light we see light.—Psalm 36:7-9 NASB

Daily Prayer

Pray along with the ***Daily Prayer*** CD. God is a God of abundance, all powerful, and all sufficient. Allow God to show you His goodness to you in the past. All God really wants is children who love Him and appreciate His lovingkindness. Notice you feel gratitude when you focus on the mercy and blessings of God.

- Practice loving and appreciating the Lord during daily activities.

Healing Prayer

Pray along with the *Healing Prayer* CD. Ask God to reveal areas where your own roots, mental strongholds, or attitudes have blocked the flow of blessing and provision that God wants to release in your life.

- Welcome the Lord to search your heart. Allow Him to remove barriers and cleanse attitudes.
- Every time a barrier is removed, you receive clarity and you can see doors of opportunity more easily.

Review of Week Three

NOTE: The *Daily Prayer* and *Healing Prayer* CDs are merely tools to help you focus and give you the benefit of a corporate anointing. Use them as long as you wish, but pray without them whenever you prefer.

1. What has the Lord has been speaking to you during the past week?

2. In which areas of weakness did you welcome an exchange of God's strength?

3. How has the love of God touched your heart this week?

4. What theme(s) have you noticed in your emotional healings?

5. What lies (if any) have been replaced by the truth? Make a list.

LIE	TRUTH

Thought for the Week

Lord Jesus, Your very nearness brings great peace within, and Your loving gaze, speaking of grace so infinite, fills my soul with joy and thankfulness. —Christian Gregor

The only bliss which we possess on earth is loving God and knowing that He loves us. —Curé d'Ars

_____

_____

_____

_____

_____

_____

_____

_____

_____

_____

_____

_____

_____

_____

_____

_____

_____

_____

_____

_____

_____

_____

Day Twenty-Two
God's Power in You

[I]t is God who is at work in you, both to will and to work for His good pleasure.—Philippians 2:13

Daily Prayer

Pray along with the ***Daily Prayer*** CD. The anointing working in you is God's power to perform. You were created by God to co-labor with Him. Yield to the power of God working within you.

_____

_____

_____

_____

_____

_____

_____

_____

_____

_____

_____

_____

_____

_____

_____

_____

_____

Healing Prayer

Pray along with the ***Healing Prayer*** CD. You not only have Christ the Forgiver living in you. He is also your Healer, Miracle Worker, Resurrection and the Life—in YOU! Any hindrance to His power is on our part, not His. What is your need? Emotional healing? Physical healing? Just be sure not to set a time limit, but know that whenever you yield to His power, change is happening in you even if you can't tell any difference right at the time.

• Ask the Lord to remove any barriers in you, and welcome His power.

Day Twenty-Three
God's Pleasure

Blessed (happy, fortunate, to be envied) is the man whose strength is in You, in whose heart are the highways to Zion. Passing through the Valley of Weeping (Baca), they make it a place of springs; the early rain also fills [the pools] with blessing.—Psalm 84:5-7 AMP

[T]he LORD takes pleasure in His people.—Psalm 149:4

Daily Prayer

Pray along with the *Daily Prayer* CD. Whenever you yield to God in prayer, you are actually touching the essence of heaven and are then able to emanate that atmosphere on earth. God takes pleasure in His people, blesses them, and releases them to bring blessing to others.

_____

_____

_____

_____

_____

_____

_____

_____

_____

_____

_____

_____

_____

Healing Prayer

Pray along with the *Healing Prayer* CD. Christ the Intercessor lives in you. And He wants to flow through you to touch others for healing, comfort, and salvation.

- Ask the Lord to remove any barriers in you that quench the anointing flowing through you to touch others.

_____

_____

_____

_____

_____

_____

_____

_____

_____

_____

_____

_____

_____

_____

_____

_____

_____

_____

_____

_____

Day Twenty-Four
God's Strength

I cling to you; your strong right hand holds me securely.—Psalm 63:8 NLT

Daily Prayer

Pray along with the ***Daily Prayer*** CD. Abandon yourself completely into God's strength; be sure that He will uphold you. He is called Immanuel, meaning "God with us," so we are never without help and you are never alone. God knows our weaknesses and is well acquainted with all our ways. He knows when we are in distress and is with us in times of trial.

_____

_____

_____

_____

_____

_____

_____

_____

_____

_____

_____

_____

_____

_____

_____

_____

Healing Prayer

Pray along with the *Healing Prayer* CD. Everyone has times of suffering in this life, but hidden roots are often the source of unnecessary trials and tribulation. Ask the Lord to search deep within your heart to remove the secret snares that trip you up.

- Invite the Lord to go anywhere He wants to bring you deliverance from bitter roots.
- If the Holy Spirit brings up an area of generational sin, feel the feeling, receive forgiveness for yourself, release forgiveness to any perpetrators, and release forgiveness back through the family line.

Day Twenty-Five
God's Loving Care

For the LORD God is a sun and shield; the LORD will give grace and glory;
No good thing will He withhold from those who walk uprightly. O LORD
of hosts, blessed is the man who trusts in You!—Psalm 84:11-12

Daily Prayer

Pray along with the ***Daily Prayer*** CD. Consider the great privilege you have in knowing that God is caring for you personally. Allow the Lord to bring to mind some of the many ways that He has been there for you when you needed Him, how He has watched over you, and provided for you.

_____

_____

_____

_____

_____

_____

_____

_____

_____

_____

_____

_____

_____

_____

Healing Prayer

Pray along with the *Healing Prayer* CD. Invite the Lord to search all areas of your life. Let go of the burdens that you have been carrying unnecessarily and welcome the tender care of the Lord. As He heals your heart, allow God to comfort you.

- Pray through roots of insecurity and fear in your life.
- Release disappointments into God's hands.

_____

_____

_____

_____

_____

_____

_____

_____

_____

_____

_____

_____

_____

_____

_____

_____

_____

_____

_____

_____

Day Twenty-Six
Divine Intimate Contact

Lean on, trust in, and be confident in the Lord with all your heart and mind and do not rely on your own insight or understanding. In all your ways know, recognize, and acknowledge [through divine intimate contact] Him, and He will direct and make straight and plain your paths.—Proverbs 3:5-6 AMP

Daily Prayer

Pray along with the *Daily Prayer* CD. Notice the word "acknowledge" in Proverbs 3:5-6. This does not mean to simply *think about* God, it means to maintain a spirit to spirit connection with Him. Feel the richness of the awareness of Christ in you. Acknowledge that He is near you and available for you whenever you need Him. As you become aware of His presence, yield even more, and welcome the increased intimacy that comes by making this Spirit to spirit connection with God.

_____

_____

_____

_____

_____

_____

_____

_____

_____

_____

_____

_____

_____

Healing Prayer

Pray along with the *Healing Prayer* CD. God has a good future planned for you and when you let the peace of God rule, He will guide you through any difficulties. You will be led by Him during times of uncertainty.

- God knows what lies ahead in your life. He is preparing you and ministering to you so that you will be ready. He knows how to orchestrate all situations.
- Receive forgiveness for impatience or insecurity and melt into His love.

_____

_____

_____

_____

_____

_____

_____

_____

_____

_____

_____

_____

_____

_____

_____

_____

_____

_____

Day Twenty-Seven
Focused on God

He who dwells in the secret place of the Most High shall abide under the shadow of the Almighty.—Psalm 91:1

Daily Prayer

Pray along with the ***Daily Prayer*** CD. Keep your entire being focused on Christ within. Welcome the presence of God saturating your entire being with His goodness. The Lord longs for you to learn to abide in Him every moment of every day. When you maintain your peace you have continual communion with the Lord. He has been searching for the one who will become a resting place for Him.

_____

_____

_____

_____

_____

_____

_____

_____

_____

_____

_____

_____

_____

_____

_____

_____

Healing Prayer

Pray along with the *Healing Prayer* CD. When you are disappointed with yourself, run *to* the Lord but not *from* Him. Come to the Lord in humility because of your great need, but not with condemnation.

- Think of yourself as a small child who comes running to your loving Father God.
- Receive forgiveness as a free gift that you do not have to earn. You merely receive it with gratitude.

_____

_____

_____

_____

_____

_____

_____

_____

_____

_____

_____

_____

_____

_____

_____

_____

_____

_____

_____

Day Twenty-Eight
Attention Increases Awareness

But let it be the inward adorning and beauty of the hidden person of the heart, with the incorruptible and unfading charm of a gentle and peaceful spirit, which [is not anxious or wrought up, but] is very precious in the sight of God.—1 Peter 3:4

Daily Prayer

Pray along with the ***Daily Prayer*** CD. Be increasingly aware of every nuance and shift—even very subtle changes. When you pay attention to the whispers of the Spirit your ability to discern increases. Notice that the anointing increases according to your focus. When you turn your gaze inward toward your Bridegroom King, it is precious to Him. He calls you His beloved, and draws closer to you whenever you turn to Him.

Healing Prayer

Pray along with the *Healing Prayer* CD. Ask the Lord for boldness to allow Him to go into dark places in your heart that you have been unconsciously avoiding. Receive forgiveness for any anxiety and know that there is great freedom on the other side of facing your fear.

- Ask the Lord to show you anything that is hindering or interfering with your ability to hear His voice.
- Receive forgiveness and allow forgiveness to flow through walls.

Review of Week Four

1. What has the Lord revealed to you this week?

2. How did the Lord bring further healing to your heart? Was there a particular pattern or theme that you noticed?

3. Remember how the Lord has been there for you, even when you didn't know that He was delighting in you, watching over you, and providing for you. The children of Israel struggled with lack of faith about God's tender care, and sometimes we do, too. Take a few minutes to remember the blessings of God.

I will bless you with a future filled with hope—a future of success, not of suffering. You will turn back to me and ask for help, and I will answer your prayers. You will worship me with all your heart, and I will be with you (Jeremiah 29:10-13 CEV).

Faithfulness in the Past	Present Trials	Future
1.	1. Look back to see how God moved on your behalf in the past.	1. God has *good* plans for you.
2.	2. He will help you overcome the trials of today.	2. Hope keeps you *open* to God's plans.
	3. God has already planned His best for your future!	
3.		
4.		
5.		
6.		

Day Twenty-Nine
Yield to the Will of God

You…are controlled not by the sinful nature but by the Spirit, if the Spirit of God lives in you. And if anyone does not have the Spirit of Christ, he does not belong to Christ. But if Christ is in you, your body is dead because of sin, yet your spirit is alive because of righteousness. And if the Spirit of him who raised Jesus from the dead is living in you, he who raised Christ from the dead will also give life to your mortal bodies through his Spirit, who lives in you.—Romans 8:9-11 NIV

Daily Prayer

Pray along with the **Daily Prayer** CD. Yield your will to the will of God. When you touch Christ in you, His life becomes your life source. This is eternal life, zoë, that comes from God Himself, and it draws you inward into a heavenly realm far beyond mere natural life. A dear saint who lived in the late 19th through the early 20th centuries had lungs which were almost destroyed by disease. Her doctors said there was no conceivable way for her to still be alive. Yet she lived for a full forty years following that grim prognosis by continuously yielding to the God life within her.

111

_____

_____

_____

Healing Prayer

Pray along with the *Healing Prayer* CD. Ask the Lord to show you issues that are hindering you from drawing closer to Him.

- Pray through a cycle and write down revelation that you receive from the Lord.
- Allow forgiveness to flow through any walls of self-protection.

_____

_____

_____

_____

_____

_____

_____

_____

_____

_____

_____

_____

_____

_____

Day Thirty
Romance of Wills

I delight to do thy will, O my God.—Psalm 40:8 KJV

Every time we dedicate our will to God in whatever happens to us, the union of love takes place.—Basilea Schlink

Daily Prayer

Pray along with the **Daily Prayer** CD. Encounter this *Romance of Wills*— God's love, your choice. Yield more fully to the flow of God's will. God's will contains all that is His very best and most perfect plan for your life. Every moment contains a gift of God's love for you if you will receive it by yielding to Him. When you insist on maintaining your peace in each circumstance of life, you receive grace, and God will cause it to work for your good and His pleasure.

_____

_____

_____

_____

_____

_____

_____

_____

_____

_____

_____

_____

_____

Healing Prayer

Pray along with the ***Healing Prayer*** CD. Invite the Lord to show you likes or dislikes that are interfering with your ability to join your will together with God's will. If there is any desire in your heart for any person, place or thing and you cannot be neutral about it, there is an unmet inner need from childhood behind it.

- Ask the Lord to show you where that got started in your life.
- Forgive whoever didn't meet that need, release demands on them, and then invite the Lord to fill the hole in your heart.
- When you feel peace, go to the Lord and present your desire before him.
- If you are truly neutral, you can be at peace so God can say either yes or no, and choose His best for you.

Day Thirty-One
A Surrendered Heart

Keep and guard your heart with all vigilance and above all that you guard, for out of it flow the springs of life.—Proverbs 4:23 AMP

Daily Prayer

Pray along with the ***Daily Prayer*** CD. Think of your heart as a castle with high walls and the will is the door of access. As soon as you open the door in prayer you connect with Christ within. Opening the heart to the Lord in prayer time is much easier than learning to keep the door open all day long. That takes practice, and we have the opportunity to do this by learning the peace walk as a lifestyle (Ephesians 6:15). Emotions are your friends, because they tell you whether or not you are abiding in God.

Healing Prayer

Pray along with the *Healing Prayer* CD. Ask the Lord to show you any hidden roots that are connected to daily events which are causing you to lose your peace.

- Allow the Lord to bring to mind people or circumstances that cause you to overreact.
- Ask the Holy Spirit to show you where that reaction got started in your life.
- Forgive God, self, and others.

_____

_____

_____

_____

_____

_____

_____

_____

_____

_____

_____

_____

_____

_____

_____

_____

_____

_____

_____

Day Thirty-Two
The Alabaster Box

Then Mary took a pound of very costly oil of spikenard, anointed the feet of Jesus, and wiped His feet with her hair. And the house was filled with the fragrance of the oil. But one of His disciples, Judas Iscariot, Simon's son, who would betray Him, said, "Why was this fragrant oil not sold for three hundred denarii and given to the poor?" This he said, not that he cared for the poor, but because he was a thief, and had the money box; and he used to take what was put in it. But Jesus said, "Let her alone; she has kept this for the day of My burial."—John 12:3-7

Daily Prayer

Pray along with the ***Daily Prayer*** CD. Yield from the place of total surrender to Christ in you. Dedicate your life, an alabaster box filled with precious perfume, to the Lord in a deeper consecration. Allow love and gratitude to flow out of your heart to your Bridegroom King. It is a fragrance which delights His heart. It is a fragrance that you can release into the atmosphere around you all day long.

_____

_____

_____

Healing Prayer

Pray along with the **_Healing Prayer_** CD. Present your heart to the Lord and allow Him to search your heart, with the request that He may have any areas not yet fully surrendered to Him.

- Pray through root issues by forgiving and releasing areas back to God.
- Invite the Lord to soften any areas where you have hardness of heart.

_____

_____

_____

_____

_____

_____

_____

_____

_____

_____

_____

_____

_____

_____

Day Thirty-Three
Total Surrender

This hope is a strong and trustworthy anchor for our souls. It leads us through the curtain [veil] into God's inner sanctuary.—Hebrews 6:19 NLT

Daily Prayer

Pray along with the ***Daily Prayer*** CD. Hebrews 6:19 encourages us to draw close to God. A veil is a barrier *in us* that separates us from God. Hope is synonymous with open. When a believer has an open heart, they are emotionally open to God, other people, and life. Any loss of hope means that you have closed your heart. Sometimes people give up because they have desires and demands that are not surrendered to God (see Day Thirty). Sometimes people shut down because they feel that they have received a promise from God, but they have waited so long, that they have stopped believing that God will bring it to pass. However, those who live a blessed life are OPEN to God's thoughts, God's emotions (the fruit of the Spirit), and God's will and ways.

_____

_____

_____

_____

_____

_____

_____

_____

_____

_____

_____

_____

_____

_____

_____

Healing Prayer

Pray along with the *Healing Prayer* CD. If you have been feeling hopeless, that is not from God. The only people who are hopeless are the unsaved who, are the only ones who are "without Christ, being aliens from the commonwealth of Israel and strangers from the covenants of promise, having no hope and without God in the world" (Ephesians 2:12).

- Allow the Lord to show you any areas of bitterness or hopelessness.
- Forgive God, self, and others and release disappointments and expectations back into the hands of God.

_____

_____

_____

_____

_____

_____

_____

_____

_____

_____

_____

_____

_____

Day Thirty-Four
Receiving

What you're after is truth from the inside out. Enter me, then; conceive a new, true life. Soak me in your laundry and I'll come out clean, scrub me and I'll have a snow white life…give me a clean bill of health. God, make a fresh start in me, shape a Genesis week from the chaos of my life.—Psalm 51:6,7,10 MSG

Daily Prayer

Pray along with the ***Daily Prayer*** CD. David wrote Psalm 51 in a time of deep repentance. Come before the Lord and ask Him to birth in you a newly intensified hunger for a new start. This is not the time to grow weary or be sidetracked, but allow the Lord to increase your dedication in pursuing more of Him through completing this Simple Prayer 60 Day Challenge. It is time to experience deeper depths in God. Write down any impression, scripture, vision while staying connected to God and taking each revelation inward presenting to God at the altar of your heart.

_____

_____

_____

_____

_____

_____

_____

_____

_____

_____

_____

_____

_____

_____

_____

Healing Prayer

Pray along with the *Healing Prayer* CD. Grace is the personal presence of Christ in you, empowering you to be all that He called you to be and do all that He called you to do! When God touches the heart, He leaves a permanent deposit of His divine nature and increased anointing. Everything that God gives you, you can release to bless others.

- Welcome the Lord to show you areas where repentance is needed and then melt into His love to receive grace for change.
- If you see a pattern of repeated failure in that area, it is attached to some root area that is chaining you to the law of sin and death. Forgiveness breaks the chain.

_____

_____

_____

_____

_____

_____

_____

_____

_____

_____

_____

_____

_____

Day Thirty-Five
Focus and Transformation

[D]o not be conformed to this world, but be transformed by the renewing of your mind [Gk. "nous"—thoughts, will, and emotions], that you may prove what is that good and acceptable and perfect will of God.—Romans 12:2

Daily Prayer

Pray along with the ***Daily Prayer*** CD. The Lord wants to bring you into perfect harmony with Him. Romans 12:2 has usually been taught to encourage believers to deal with the thought life, and that this practice alone would bring transformation. However, the word *mind* in the Greek is *nous*, which actually means the total being that includes *thoughts, will, and emotions*. This means that all three elements must be renewed for a believer to be transformed.

_____

_____

_____

_____

_____

_____

_____

_____

_____

_____

_____

_____

_____

_____

_____

_____

_____

_____

_____

Healing Prayer

Pray along with the *Healing Prayer* CD. As you focus on Christ within this allows the Spirit to penetrate the depths of the heart.

- Allow the light of the Lord to search your heart for any patterns of thinking, emotions, or choices that need transformation.

_____

_____

_____

_____

_____

_____

_____

_____

_____

_____

_____

_____

_____

_____

_____

_____

Review of Week Five

1. Have you been praying/talking to an accountability partner on a regular basis? If you don't have one perhaps you should ask the Lord about finding one for you.

   ☐ Yes
   ☐ No
   ☐ No, but I plan to ask _____ to be a partner.

2. Have you considered finding a disciple to share what you have been learning? Perhaps God wants you to become a prayer mentor to help someone else.

3. What revelation have you received from the Lord this past week?

4. What scripture verses have been quickened to you?

5. In what ways has your life changed for the better since you began the Challenge?

6. How have you grown closer to the Lord?

Thought for the Week

Only in times of quiet, away from the hustle and bustle of daily life, with nothing and no one to distract us, can Jesus give us His love more fully and more intimately.... Let us be faithful in our quiet times, keeping them holy for Him.—Balilea Schlink

Day Thirty-Six
Precious and Weighty Thoughts

How precious and weighty also are Your thoughts to me, O God! How vast is the sum of them!—Psalm 139:17 AMP

Daily Prayer

Pray along with the ***Daily Prayer*** CD. Every word from God is more priceless than all the treasures in the world. Cherish each nugget the Lord gives you as precious and weighty, of infinite value. Receive every word, truth, picture, and impression. Don't just think about it, but hold it in your heart, write it down without leaving His presence, and immediately return to Him.

_____

_____

_____

_____

_____

_____

_____

_____

_____

_____

_____

_____

_____

_____

_____

Healing Prayer

Pray along with the *Healing Prayer* CD. Invite the Lord to search all areas of your life. As He heals your heart, allow God to minister to you and give you fresh revelation.

- Pray through roots that have hindered you from hearing God clearly. Forgive God, self, and others.
- Repent for letting revelation pass unnoticed. Ask God to restore precious gems of truth that were lost.

_____

_____

_____

_____

_____

_____

_____

_____

_____

_____

_____

_____

_____

_____

_____

_____

_____

_____

_____

_____

_____

_____

Day Thirty-Seven
Growth and Increase

So then neither he who plants is anything, nor he who waters, but God who gives the increase.—1 Corinthians 3:7

Daily Prayer

Pray along with the ***Daily Prayer*** CD. Every revelation from the heart of God to man is full of His love, and its life source is derived from God Himself. When it is planted in the heart, it will grow. How carefully we tend it determines how much it will grow, but it is God who gives the increase. Welcome the presence of God to show you something that He wants you to pay attention to so that it will grow in your life.

_____

_____

_____

_____

_____

_____

_____

_____

_____

_____

_____

_____

_____

Healing Prayer

Pray along with the *Healing Prayer* CD. Invite the Lord to search your heart for roots or bad attitudes that may be hindering the increase that He wants to bring into your life.

- Pray through roots that have caused lack of increase.
- Forgive God, self, and others.

_____

_____

_____

_____

_____

_____

_____

_____

_____

_____

_____

_____

_____

_____

_____

_____

_____

_____

_____

_____

_____

Day Thirty-Eight
Seeds

The kingdom of God is as if a man should scatter seed on the ground, and should sleep by night and rise by day, and the seed should sprout and grow, he himself does not know how. For the earth yields crops by itself: first the blade, then the head, after that the full grain in the head.—Mark 4:26-29

Daily Prayer

Pray along with the ***Daily Prayer*** CD. Welcome every impression, scripture or vision to grow and increase from the place of union and communion. Stay in prayer and the Lord will cause that revelation to grow. Everything that comes from God has life in it, and it will grow if you just let God bring the increase. Dennis and I allow these precious God thoughts to develop and grow, and discover that they grow into sermons, teachings, strategies to help others, and eventually dreams to be fulfilled. Ask the Lord to share a weighty and precious thought with you now, and write it down.

_____

_____

_____

_____

_____

_____

_____

_____

_____

_____

_____

_____

_____

_____

_____

_____

Healing Prayer

Pray along with the ***Healing Prayer*** CD. Allow God to plow up any hard ground in your heart to make it more receptive for revelation to take root and grow.

- Let the Lord search your heart for areas where there is hard ground, thorns (cares of this life), or stony places that have blocked growth.

_____

_____

_____

_____

_____

_____

_____

_____

_____

_____

_____

_____

_____

_____

_____

SECTION FIVE

DAYS 39–60

Functions of Your Spirit

Day Thirty-Nine
Rivers of Living Water

IV. FUNCTIONS OF YOUR SPIRIT

FORGIVING

[W]hoever drinks of the water that I shall give him will never thirst. But the water that I shall give him will become in him a fountain of water springing up into everlasting life.—John 4:14

He that believeth on me, as the scripture hath said, out of his belly shall flow rivers of living water.—John 7:38 KJV

Daily Prayer

Pray along with the ***Daily Prayer*** CD. **There are four primary functions of your human spirit: forgiving, loving, releasing, and receiving.** Each one depends on yielding the heart to God, because He is the source of all good things. **Forgiveness** is the gift Jesus gave us to remove barriers between God and man, and man to man. As you yield and Christ forgives through you, a river of living water flows out from the deepest part of your innermost being, your heart, the seat of your emotions. Freely release rivers of forgiveness in advance to whoever may offend during the day.

_____

_____

_____

_____

_____

_____

_____

_____

_____

_____

_____

_____

_____

Healing Prayer

Pray along with the *Healing Prayer* CD. Allow forgiveness to flow freely to whoever God shows you. You did nothing to earn it, so give as freely as you received.

- Deal with every person and situation that the Lord reveals to you.
- Release forgiveness to God, self, and others.

_____

_____

_____

_____

_____

_____

_____

_____

_____

_____

_____

_____

_____

_____

_____

_____

Day Forty
Flow of Love

You are a fountain [springing up] in a garden, a well of living waters, and flowing streams from Lebanon. [You have called me a garden, she said] Oh, I pray that the…north wind and the…south wind may blow upon my garden that its spices may flow out [in abundance for you in whom my soul delights]. Let my beloved come into his garden and eat its choicest fruits.
—Song of Solomon 4:15-16 AMP

Daily Prayer

Pray along with the *Daily Prayer* CD. You can give to others whatever you have received from God. The whole world needs the forgiveness and the love of God. Allow the love of God to flow out to others during the day.

_____

_____

_____

_____

_____

_____

_____

_____

_____

_____

_____

_____

_____

_____

Healing Prayer

Pray along with the *Healing Prayer* CD. Allow the Lord to show you any areas where you have been blocking the flow of His anointing in your life.

- Release forgiveness to every person that the Lord reveals to you.

_____

_____

_____

_____

_____

_____

_____

_____

_____

_____

_____

_____

_____

_____

_____

_____

_____

_____

_____

_____

Day Forty-One
Life and Healing

And it shall be that every living thing that moves, wherever the rivers go, will live. There will be a very great multitude of fish, because these waters go there; for they will be healed, and everything will live wherever the river goes.—Ezekiel 47:9

Daily Prayer

Pray along with the **Daily Prayer** CD. Practice loving forgiveness again today. Notice that whenever you are releasing love you experience a deep sense of satisfaction. When you allow love to flow out to others who are hurting, you are releasing the compassion of Christ. Multiple times in the Gospels, we read that miracles occurred when the heart of Jesus was moved with compassion. Release forgiveness like a river and wherever it goes forth it brings life.

_____

_____

_____

_____

_____

_____

_____

_____

_____

_____

_____

_____

_____

_____

Healing Prayer

Pray along with the *Healing Prayer* CD. If we don't get our way with people, we often react to them as they are inanimate objects depriving us of what we deserve. Whenever we are frustrated or impatient with circumstances, we are really angry at God. He didn't do anything wrong, but the sinful human nature likes the world to revolve around selfish desires and personal convenience. In Matthew 5:21-22, Jesus says, "I'm telling you that anyone who is so much as angry with a brother or sister is guilty of murder."

- Receive forgiveness for judging God, and forgive Him for things that might not go as you wish during the day.
- Release forgiveness in advance to people.

Day Forty-Two
Forgive in Advance

Don't grieve God. Don't break his heart. His Holy Spirit, moving and breathing in you, is the most intimate part of your life, making you fit for himself. Don't take such a gift for granted. Make a clean break with all cutting, backbiting, profane talk. Be gentle with one another, sensitive. Forgive one another as quickly and thoroughly as God in Christ forgave you.—Ephesians 4:30-32 MSG

Daily Prayer

Pray along with the ***Daily Prayer*** CD. Forgive in advance all offenses that will come today. Christ the Forgiver lives in you, and He already knows what will happen. He already paid the price for the sins of the ones who will wound you, disrespect you, and make you angry today. You will please Him so much if you forgive just as He forgave, before it ever even happened.

_____

_____

_____

Healing Prayer

Pray along with the *Healing Prayer* CD. Invite the Lord to show you the "little things" which grieve His heart but you yourself overlook.

- Allow God to deal with complaining and ingratitude toward Him.
- Let God cleanse your heart of judgments toward the body of Christ.

_____

_____

_____

_____

_____

_____

_____

_____

_____

_____

_____

_____

_____

_____

_____

_____

Review of Week Six

1. What are the main thoughts that the Lord has been speaking to your heart? List a few of them here.

2. What scripture verses had special life to them?

3. What theme(s) have you noticed in your emotional healings?

4. What changes have you noticed in your life since Day One?

Thought for the Week

Because we are the most forgiven people in the world, we should be the most forgiving people in the world.—C. J. Mahaney[1]

_____

_____

_____

_____

_____

_____

_____

_____

_____

_____

_____

_____

_____

_____

_____

_____

_____

_____

_____

_____

1. Mahaney, C. J. (2002). *Pastoral Leadership for Manhood and Womanhood*, ed. Wayne Grudem and Dennis Rainey, Crossway. 202.

Day Forty-Three
Forgive in Advance

Then Peter came to [Jesus] and said, "Lord, how often shall my brother sin against me, and I forgive him? Up to seven times?" Jesus said to him, "I do not say to you, up to seven times, but up to seventy times seven."—Matthew 18:21

Daily Prayer

Pray along with the ***Daily Prayer*** CD. Release forgiveness to those with whom you come in contact with today. Whenever you are tempted to be offended, allow a river of forgiveness to flow out before you respond in any negative way.

Healing Prayer

Pray along with the *Healing Prayer* CD. Love and forgive both friend and foe. Jesus said that we are no better than the unsaved if we only love those who love us. 46 percent of all Christians no longer go to church because they were hurt in church. The main reason they isolate themselves is their failure to forgive. Have you allowed the Lord to adjust your attitude toward pastors and church members who have misunderstood you, judged you, wounded, or embarrassed you in the past?

- Welcome the Holy Spirit to go deep into the dark places to set you free from the walls of fear that you hide behind.

_____

_____

_____

_____

_____

_____

_____

_____

_____

_____

_____

_____

_____

_____

_____

_____

_____

Day Forty-Four
Grace and Power

LOVING

He showed me the river whose waters give life, sparkling like crystal, flowing out from the throne of God and of the Lamb through the middle of the broad way of the city; also, on either side of the river was the tree of life with its twelve varieties of fruit, yielding each month its fresh crop; and the leaves of the tree were for the healing and the restoration of the nations.
—Revelation 22:1-2

Daily Prayer

Pray along with the *Daily Prayer* CD. The purpose for your creation and salvation was that you might love God. You have been given the amazing privilege to love the God who is Love. The world was created by love and redeemed by love. And Jesus, the One who died for you, wants you to love Him as a bride loves her bridegroom, forsaking all other loves for her Beloved. Just think. That is all Jesus really wants you to do. And in loving Him above all else, love becomes your motivation and your teacher. Love is so powerful that it breaks through the walls in the hearts of people. Practice going to the supermarket, workplace, or church dinner and emanate loving without words. Many times people will be drawn to you and not understand why.

_____

_____

_____

_____

_____

_____

_____

_____

_____

_____

_____

_____

Healing Prayer

Pray along with the *Healing Prayer* CD. Come before the Lord with gratitude for all that He is doing in your life. Allow the Lord to search the hidden places for hurts, fears, shame, and angers. Allow Him to go deeper still to deal with roots to more subtle forms of anger such as frustration and impatience.

- Ask the Lord to heal the hurts and fears in your heart that keep you from knowing His love for you, and prevent you from loving Him as fervently as you desire.

_____

_____

_____

_____

_____

_____

_____

_____

_____

_____

_____

_____

_____

Day Forty-Five
Loving Intercession

Beloved, let us love one another, for love is of God; and everyone who loves is born of God and knows God.—1 John 4:7

Daily Prayer

Pray along with the ***Daily Prayer*** CD. Let a river of love flow out to family, loved ones, and those that the Lord brings to mind. Love is a powerful spiritual force, and there is no distance in the spirit. If you release love from the belly to a dear friend on the mission field in Africa or India, they can often sense that someone is praying for them. If you are concerned about your child who is away on a trip, your loving intercession is actually releasing divine intervention to work on his or her behalf.

Healing Prayer

Pray along with the *Healing Prayer* CD. Trust is the foundation of all relationships, and fear or insecurity in your relationship with God indicates a need for healing in this area. He knows that we cannot change ourselves, so we hide from God and one another. We are all ensnared in our past wounds and sinful nature unless His love sets us free. The walls of childhood become the traps of adulthood.

- Let God go anywhere in your heart and forgive as He leads.
- If you felt any fear or doubt that God would work as you pray, allow God to deal with any root issues of trust.

Day Forty-Six
River of Love

I am my beloved's, And my beloved is mine.—Song of Solomon 6:3

Daily Prayer

Pray along with the *Daily Prayer* CD. Yield to God's love toward you, and allow love to flow back to Him. Do you long for more of this great love? If the Lord has placed this desire in your heart, your prayer will surely be answered. Now allow loving intercession to flow out on behalf of others.

_____

_____

_____

_____

_____

_____

_____

_____

_____

_____

_____

_____

_____

_____

_____

_____

_____

Healing Prayer

Pray along with the *Healing Prayer* CD. Welcome the Lord to search in all the secret recesses of your heart. Run to His love and His light, and allow Him to expose and cleanse hidden wounds and toxic attitudes.

• Forgive God, self and others.

_____

_____

_____

_____

_____

_____

_____

_____

_____

_____

_____

_____

_____

_____

_____

_____

_____

_____

_____

_____

Day Forty-Seven
Blessing

But I say unto you, Love your enemies, bless them that curse you, do good to them that hate you, and pray for them which despitefully use you, and persecute you.—Matthew 5:44

Daily Prayer

Pray along with the ***Daily Prayer*** CD. Allow a river of loving intercession to flow to your loved ones before you open your mouth to say, "Lord, bless them and keep them." Forgive those who have harmed you. The Lord will protect you and deal with them. Know that God is at work even if you can't see it. Work on yourself and leave others in the hands of God. *"When a man's ways please the LORD, He makes even his enemies to be at peace with him"* (Proverbs 16:7).

Healing Prayer

Pray along with the *Healing Prayer* CD. Release difficult people into the hands of God until you feel peace. When you deal with your own heart, the Lord will deal with those who have been your enemies in His way and His time.

- Release yourself to the Lord, so that you don't try to keep yourself safe, but allow Him to guard you through peace.
- Place your possessions and reputation into God's hands for safekeeping.

_____

_____

_____

_____

_____

_____

_____

_____

_____

_____

_____

_____

_____

_____

_____

_____

_____

_____

_____

Day Forty-Eight
A Fountain Springing Up

RELEASING

But he who trusts in the LORD, lovingkindness shall surround him.
—Psalm 32:10 NASB

Daily Prayer

Pray along with the ***Daily Prayer*** CD. Release people and circumstances into the hands of God. Trust Him to do what is impossible for you. Release husbands, wives, children, coworkers, friends, and whoever comes to mind. Let an artesian well of living water flow from your heart. Practice this in your prayer time, but continue to trust God all during the day.

Healing Prayer

Pray along with the *Healing Prayer* CD. Allow the Lord to go deep in your heart to heal wounds, fine tune your attitudes, set you free, and open wells that need uncapping.

- If you think of a painful memory, remember that you were afraid, but feel numb, receive forgiveness for letting fear guard you, then pray through the issue until you get peace.
- If you have a place where you retreat into yourself when you are afraid, receive forgiveness for the fear and welcome the Lord to flood that area and surround you with His presence.

_____

_____

_____

_____

_____

_____

_____

_____

_____

_____

_____

_____

_____

_____

_____

_____

_____

Day Forty-Nine
"Let it Go"

Give all your worries and cares to God, for he cares about you.—1 Peter 5:7 NLT

Daily Prayer

Pray along with the *Daily Prayer* CD. **Release** all the people and situations that cause you to worry into the hands of God. This applies to circumstances, schedules, demands and expectations. Fretting doesn't cause the answers to come any sooner; it just prevents you from enjoying today.

_____

_____

_____

_____

_____

_____

_____

_____

_____

_____

_____

_____

_____

_____

_____

_____

_____

_____

Healing Prayer

Pray along with the *Healing Prayer* CD. Our insecurity causes us to doubt the goodness of God. The serpent tricked Eve in the book of Genesis by stirring up suspicion that the Lord was holding back something good from her.

- Welcome the Lord to search your heart for root issues connected to being suspicious of God's intentions toward you.
- When you have prayed that through, release people and circumstances back into the hands of a loving God.

_____

_____

_____

_____

_____

_____

_____

_____

_____

_____

_____

_____

_____

_____

_____

_____

_____

Review of Week Seven

1. What are the main thoughts that the Lord has been speaking to your heart?

2. Write one or two of the scriptures that stand out. Why?

3. What have you released to the Lord this past week?

4. How have you been successful in walking in peace in your daily life? Every baby step of obedience builds spiritual strength so rejoice in even small victories.

Thought for the Week

"Bridal love for Jesus is nourished and grows when we daily bind ourselves to Him. The dedication of the will leads us into the deepest union of love with Jesus. The true test of bridal love is the willingness to submit wholly to the will of God, even when He frustrates our dearest wishes or we cannot understand what He is doing either in our lives or in the lives of others. To nurture bridal love and to show Jesus that we love Him, we need constantly to practice submitting to His will and wishes.... The time has come for the genuineness of my love to be tested.... I can prove my love for Him by loving His will."—Basilea Schlink[1]

_____

_____

_____

_____

_____

_____

_____

_____

_____

_____

_____

_____

_____

_____

_____

_____

_____

_____

1. Schlink, B. (1969). *My All for Him*. Bloomington, MN: Bethany Press International. 77–78.

Day Fifty
Let Go and Let God

Lean on, trust in, and be confident in the Lord with all your heart and mind and do not rely on your own insight or understanding. In all your ways know, recognize, and acknowledge [divine intimate contact] Him, and He will direct and make straight and plain your paths.—Proverbs 3:5-6 AMP

Daily Prayer

Pray along with the ***Daily Prayer*** CD. You cannot trust God and be stressed at the same time. In the Hebrew, one definition of *trust* is *to make someone your refuge.* When you feel tense, notice how you feel in the belly. It feels tight, not relaxed and open, and the emotion is mild anxiety or worse. That means that you are holding on. When you release a person or circumstance to God, you are not letting go into nothingness, but into the most powerful, trustworthy, and loving hands in the universe.

_____

_____

_____

_____

_____

_____

_____

_____

_____

_____

_____

Healing Prayer

Pray along with the *Healing Prayer* CD. Out of your innermost being, through the connection of Christ within, from that place of TRUST let go and let God.

- Release all control of circumstances, deadlines, schedules back into the hand of God.
- Welcome God to search your heart for roots that are interfering with your trust for God today.
- Forgive, release demands, and allow God to fill in areas of need, such as for approval, love, affirmation, and security.

Day Fifty-One
Wait for God

I waited patiently for the LORD; And He inclined to me, and heard my cry.—Psalm 40:1

Daily Prayer

Pray along with the *Daily Prayer* CD. Yield to God's timetable not yours. God is never too early, and He is never too late. Release your schedule into the loving cadence of the Lord.

Healing Prayer

Pray along with the *Healing Prayer* CD. If waiting for God to bring promises to pass has been a difficult area in your life, welcome Him to go into the dark places in your heart and heal wounds, but also deal with roots of insecurity and impatience.

- Allow forgiveness to flow to God, self, and others.
- Let go of anything you have been clinging to.

Day Fifty-Two
Release Demands and Expectations

They are God's servants, not yours. They are responsible to Him, not to you. Let Him tell them whether they are right or wrong. And God is able to make them do as they should.—Romans 14:4 TLB

Daily Prayer

Pray along with the ***Daily Prayer*** CD. **Release** demands and expectations on people. Release what you want them to do that they are not doing, and what you do not want them to do. Release demands that you put on yourself. *You* too belong to God and not yourself.

_____

_____

_____

_____

_____

_____

_____

_____

_____

_____

_____

_____

_____

_____

_____

_____

Healing Prayer

Pray along with the *Healing Prayer* CD. Continue to welcome God to search your heart for situations where you felt forced to take control, your parents put too much responsibility on you, or it made you feel good to be the rescuer for others. Allow God to go to the root.

- Receive forgiveness, release forgiveness.
- Release demands and expectations on yourself back to God.

_____

_____

_____

_____

_____

_____

_____

_____

_____

_____

_____

_____

_____

_____

_____

_____

_____

_____

Day Fifty-Three
Release Yourself to God

[You] are God's servants, not [your own]. [You] are responsible to Him, not to you. Let Him tell [you] whether [you] are right or wrong. And God is able to make [you] do as [you] should.—Romans 14:4 TLB

Daily Prayer

Pray along with the ***Daily Prayer*** CD. "God's kingdom come, His will be done (not yours), on earth as it is in heaven." Release demands and expectations back into the capable hands of God. Release yourself to God. *You* are God's servant, not your own. *You* belong to Him and not to *you*. Stay in prayer and let the Lord saturate you with this truth.

_____

_____

_____

_____

_____

_____

_____

_____

_____

_____

_____

_____

_____

_____

_____

Healing Prayer

Pray along with the *Healing Prayer* CD. Do you ever feel frustrated with yourself in your Christian life? Have you secretly judged yourself, that maybe you are not spiritual enough, or diligent enough? Those are standards of your own making. God wants you to leave your spiritual progress up to Him.

- Receive forgiveness for living by a man-made standard that is not the standard of the Cross.
- Allow the Lord to heal heart wounds that are contributing to your frustration.

Day Fifty-Four
Receive God's Care

RECEIVING

If God gives such attention to the appearance of wildflowers—most of which are never even seen—don't you think He'll attend to you, take pride in you, do His best for you? What I'm trying to do here is to get you to relax, to not be so preoccupied with getting, so you can respond to God's giving. People who don't know God and the way He works fuss over these things, but you know both God and how he works. Steep your life in God-reality, God-initiative, God-provisions. Don't worry about missing out. You'll find all your everyday human concerns will be met.—Matthew 16:32-33 MSG

Daily Prayer

Pray along with the ***Daily Prayer*** CD. Learn to function from your spirit in **receiving**. This is the next loving function of your spirit. In receiving, you are yielding, drinking in, absorbing. In your prayer time, pay attention to the sense of God's presence and yield to Him.

_____

_____

_____

_____

_____

_____

_____

_____

_____

_____

_____

_____

_____

_____

Healing Prayer

Pray along with the **Healing Prayer** CD. *"Lord, help me cultivate a more implicit trust in you. I choose to live a life of God worship. Please set me free to love you more fully."*

- Receive forgiveness for failure to trust.
- Forgive those who failed to be trustworthy in your life.

_____

_____

_____

_____

_____

_____

_____

_____

_____

_____

_____

_____

_____

_____

_____

Day Fifty-Five
Bridegroom King

I found the one I love. I held him and would not let him go.—Song of Solomon 3:4

The bride… looks glorious in her golden gown. In her beautiful robes, she is led to the king, accompanied by her bridesmaids. What a joyful and enthusiastic procession as they enter the king's palace!—Psalm 45:13-15 NLT

Daily Prayer

Pray along with the *Daily Prayer* CD. Jesus wants you to know Him not only as your Savior, or your Provider, He wants to know you as your beloved—your Bridegroom King. As He reveals Himself to you, receive whatever He quickens to you as pure gold.

_____

_____

_____

_____

_____

_____

_____

_____

_____

_____

_____

_____

_____

_____

_____

_____

Healing Prayer

Pray along with the *Healing Prayer* CD. Welcome the Lord to search the inner recesses of your heart for other loves that are competing with His love.

- Receive forgiveness, welcome the work of the cross, lay other loves at His feet, and allow Him to take His place in your heart.

_____

_____

_____

_____

_____

_____

_____

_____

_____

_____

_____

_____

_____

_____

Day Fifty-Six
Time in God's Presence

But one thing is needed, and Mary has chosen that good part, which will not be taken away from her.—Luke 10:42

Daily Prayer

Pray along with the ***Daily Prayer*** CD. *"Come away, My Beloved."* You never waste a moment in prayer. You never waste time in the presence of God. Allow whatever the Lord has shown you to be incubated so it can grow.

_____

_____

_____

_____

_____

_____

_____

_____

_____

_____

_____

_____

_____

_____

_____

_____

_____

Healing Prayer

Pray along with the *Healing Prayer* CD. Invite the Lord to search your heart for anything hindering the divine romance that He wants to have with you.

- Forgive God, self, and others.

_____

_____

_____

_____

_____

_____

_____

_____

_____

_____

_____

_____

_____

_____

_____

_____

_____

_____

_____

_____

Review of Week Eight

1. What are the main thoughts that the Lord has been speaking to your heart?

2. Write one or two of the scriptures that stand out. Why?

3. What difficulties have you overcome?

4. What theme(s) have you noticed in your emotional healings?

5. What are some things that used to bother you, but don't anymore?

Thought for the Week

Seven Benefits of Forgiveness

1. You please God.
2. You feel better inside.
3. You can live in the fruit of the spirit.
4. You grow emotionally.
5. You make better decisions with peace.
6. You are anointed to be a blessing to others.
7. You have better health.

Day Fifty-Seven
Motivated by Love

Christ's love has moved me to such extremes. His love has the first and last word in everything we do.—2 Corinthians 5:13 MSG

Daily Prayer

Pray along with the *Daily Prayer* CD. Just as you have welcomed Christ's love for you, now focus on your love flowing back to Him. Jesus gave Himself completely for you. His love has been healing your heart and removing barriers so that you can know His love, and you can return love back to Him. Let this love be the motivation behind all your obedience and service to Him. Focus on Christ within you. Receive, cherish, absorb, honor, and welcome any word or impression He gives.

_____

_____

_____

_____

_____

_____

_____

_____

_____

_____

_____

_____

_____

_____

_____

Healing Prayer

Pray along with the *Healing Prayer* CD. Ask the Lord to reveal any personal opinion or preference no matter how small that is blocking your flow of love.

- Receive forgiveness and forgive others.
- Release your ideas and desires to God, and ask Him for His ideas and desires.

_____

_____

_____

_____

_____

_____

_____

_____

_____

_____

_____

_____

_____

_____

_____

_____

_____

_____

Day Fifty-Eight
Living Epistles

Clearly you are an epistle of Christ, ministered by us, written not with ink but by the Spirit of the living God, not on tablets of stone but on tablets of flesh, that is, of the heart.—2 Corinthians 3:3

Daily Prayer

Pray along with the *Daily Prayer* CD. When God touches you He leaves an imprint of His nature of your spirit. Allow it to be written of your heart in ever deepening truth.

Healing Prayer

Pray along with the *Healing Prayer* CD. Ask the Lord to show you any words or beliefs about yourself which have left a negative imprint on your life. Often these words form part of a false identity or personality that blocks the expression of the New Creation.

- Allow the Lord to show you where any false identity came in.
- Forgive whoever said it, including yourself, receive forgiveness for taking it in, renounce it, then ask the Lord to tell you what He says about who you really are.
- Write down what God says to you!

_____

_____

_____

_____

_____

_____

_____

_____

_____

_____

_____

_____

_____

_____

_____

_____

_____

_____

Day Fifty-Nine
Reality

Write these commandments that I've given you today on your hearts. Get them inside of you and then get them inside your children. Talk about them wherever you are, sitting at home or walking in the street; talk about them from the time you get up in the morning to when you fall into bed at night. Tie them on your hands and foreheads as a reminder; inscribe them on the doorposts of your homes and on your city gates.—Deuteronomy 6:9 MSG

Daily Prayer

Pray along with the ***Daily Prayer*** CD. Whatever God writes on your heart touches your entire being. Even the cells of your physical body are changed by His love. Welcome Him into every organ and system.

_____

_____

_____

_____

_____

_____

_____

_____

_____

_____

_____

_____

_____

_____

_____

_____

Healing Prayer

Pray along with the *Healing Prayer* CD. Welcome the presence of God, Christ the Healer within, to saturate your entire being, every cell of your body, with His reality.

- Pray through forgiveness until you get peace.
- Do not beg for healing, but receive it and welcome the flow of healing anointing from Christ the Healer in you.

_____

_____

_____

_____

_____

_____

_____

_____

_____

_____

_____

_____

_____

_____

_____

_____

_____

_____

_____

_____

Day Sixty
No Barriers

May He grant you out of the rich treasury of His glory to be strengthened and reinforced with mighty power in the inner man by the [Holy] Spirit [Himself indwelling your innermost being and personality]. May Christ through your faith [actually] dwell (settle down, abide, make His permanent home) in your hearts! May you be rooted deep in love and founded securely on love, That you may have the power and be strong to apprehend and grasp with all the saints [God's devoted people, the experience of that love] what is the breadth and length and height and depth [of it]; [That you may really come] to know [practically, through experience for yourselves] the love of Christ, which far surpasses mere knowledge [without experience]; that you may be filled [through all your being] unto all the fullness of God [may have the richest measure of the divine Presence, and become a body wholly filled and flooded with God Himself]!—Ephesians 3:16-19 AMP

Daily Prayer

Pray along with the *Daily Prayer* CD. Don't let ANYTHING come between what you and the Lord have together. He rejoices over you. Delight in the precious moments that you spend with Him because you are His beloved! Draw near to Him. You have everything you need…**because everything you need is in Him!**

_____

_____

_____

_____

_____

_____

_____

_____

_____

_____

_____

_____

_____

Healing Prayer

Pray along with the *Healing Prayer* CD. Allow the Lord to show you any barriers that are keeping you from going deeper in Him. *"Lord, I have begun a brand new journey with You, and I am hungry for even more. Lead me into more of your love and glory than I can even imagine!"*

- Receive forgiveness for yourself, and forgive God and others.
- Allow forgiveness to flow through barriers or walls of unbelief.
- Receive, absorb, and drink in all that God has given to you during the *60-Day Challenge.*

_____

_____

_____

_____

_____

_____

_____

_____

_____

_____

_____

_____

Review of Sixty Days

I will betroth you to Me forever; yes, I will betroth you to Me in righteousness and justice, in lovingkindness and mercy; I will betroth you to Me in faithfulness, and you shall know the LORD.—Hosea 2:19-20

1. How has the *60-Day Emotional Healing Challenge* changed your relationship with God?

2. What promises have you received from the Lord?

3. What changes have you noticed in yourself?

4. What changes have other people noticed in you?

5. What are some of the most significant revelations that you have received from the Lord?

NOTES